OVERCOMING INFERTILITY

HAMLYN HELP YOURSELF GUIDE

OVERCOMING INFERTILITY

DR. GRAHAM H. BARKER

HAMLYN

First published as *The New Fertility* in 1986 by
Adamson Books
Akeman House, High Street, Stretham,
Ely, Cambridgeshire CB6 3JQ

This abridged edition published in 1990 by
The Hamlyn Publishing Group Limited,
a division of the Octopus Publishing Group,
Michelin House, 81 Fulham Road,
London SW3 6RB

ISBN 0 600 56903 9

Illustrations Jennie Smith

Printed and bound in Great Britain
by Collins, Glasgow

Contents

Foreword
to the original edition

The investigations and treatments now available to a couple who have difficulty in having a child have been greatly advanced and improved over the past decade. It is not easy for every couple to understand the normal processes involved in conception and the many ways in which problems occur, and their necessary remedies. Doctors and other workers involved with fertility treatments are unable to give each couple a complete and thorough explanation of the complex processes and treatments at each consultation. Yet a couple's understanding of these processes and treatments will greatly help both themselves and their doctors and, of course, reduce stress and anxiety on all sides. This book aims to explain fertility problems and their treatment in a helpful, sympathetic and detailed way, and I hope its readers will greatly benefit from the understanding they derive from it.

PATRICK STEPTOE CBE, FRS, FRCS, FRCOG (1913–1988)
Late Director, Bourn Hall Clinic,
Bourn, Cambridge

Preface

Any couple who, either temporarily or permanently, are unable to have children when they wish to face many problems – emotional, psychological, and possibly medical. They frequently experience frustration, anger and bewilderment at the relative complexity of infertility, its investigation and possible treatment. Having children seems to be such a natural thing for most people, it is difficult to come to terms with the fact that when things go wrong they can be extraordinarily difficult to put right.

The aim of this book is to answer as many questions as possible about infertility, so that you can approach your treatment with confidence rather than anxiety. It is primarily designed for those of you who are just starting your infertility investigations or think you might need medical help. I hope to guide you along the path that the average series of investigations and treatments takes, so that with each chapter your knowledge increases gradually.

In infertility, unlike illness, you will be consulting a doctor for assistance when you are essentially healthy, and you will be taking great interest in the tests and procedures which are on offer. Having this book on hand will, I hope, make consultations and co-operation between you as a couple and your doctor more rewarding.

I wanted to write this book right from my early training in gynaecology – ever since, in fact, I first tried to explain to infertile patients what our complex tests and treatments involved and meant. Originally published in 1986 in a more detailed version by Adamson Books, this new, up-dated but simplified edition will, I hope, continue to bring information and reassurance to thousands of hopeful couples.

GRAHAM H. BARKER TD, AKC, MB, BS, FRCS, MRCOG
London, 1990

ONE

Thinking about infertility

It is estimated that some 10 per cent of all couples in Europe experience a period of infertility, and as many as 8 per cent of marriages remain childless after ten years. It may be true that we live in an age where the increase in world population is a cause for concern, that there is a growing acceptance that the careers of certain couples might preclude children, and that consequently the emphasis on parenthood as the natural product of marriage has declined. Nevertheless, the desire to have children is deeply rooted and represents for most people a means of emotional fulfilment and a natural expression of love.

The couple who cannot have children when they want to often feel enormous sadness and frustration. Added to this, social and family pressures are often still very strong: newly-weds still commence their married life among ancient fertility rites such as rose-petal and rice throwing. History and literature are littered with stories and events which revolve round childbirth and inheritance, so, like it or not, the young couple today will need a thick skin before announcing to potential grandparents that they have decided not to have a family.

Overcoming stress
If you find yourselves unable to conceive in this climate, you may well find yourselves under stress from the start, with a mixed feeling of guilt and mistrust. To minimize the build-up of stress – which can only aggravate the problem – it is essential

that you should have your difficulty investigated and treated as early as possible.

No discussion of fertility can leave aside the connection between a happy marriage and parenthood. On the one hand, many marriages – or close relationships – have been stabilized by the addition of a child (though parenthood is by no means a panacea for all marital ills). On the other hand, psychological stresses produced by discord between a couple can delay conception – in obvious ways such as by interrupting the pattern and frequency of intercourse, and more subtle ways, such as an unconscious, anxiety-induced inhibition of conception. It is difficult to find an explanation for the psychological causes of infertility, but they do seem to exist: many couples who have experienced serious marital problems accompanied by infertility have found no difficulty in conceiving during subsequent periods of relative calm and relaxation.

Please do not think that I am trying to suggest that all problems of infertility are 'in the mind'. They are not, and all infertile couples should be properly and scientifically investigated if they wish. Nevertheless the psychological aspect is extremely important in some cases – as most people working in this field can testify. Many couples conceive soon after infertility investigations have begun, perhaps because they can relax in the reassuring knowledge that their problem is being looked at. All practitioners have stories to tell of couples 'barren' for many years who suddenly find themselves proud expectant parents after only a couple of preliminary visits to the infertility clinic. It is equally common to find normal couples who have not used contraception but whose children are well spaced out, with several years between each.

Time factors

There is a lot of variation in the speed with which couples are able to produce children, and this is not surprising when we consider the many complex factors and interactions required to initiate and sustain a pregnancy. Some women become pregnant almost as soon as contraceptive precautions are abandoned, while others wait several years before the first child is born. Mutual and individual fertility varies throughout life but, in general, a woman's fertility tends to decline towards the end of her reproductive years, particularly after the age of 40, although pregnancies in women approaching 50 and even beyond are occasionally reported. The pattern in men is not so well defined and a man's reproductive life may well extend into very old age.

Potency and fertility

There is an important distinction to make between infertility – the inability of a woman to conceive a child or of a man to father a child – and impotence, which is a man's inability to perform the sexual act. Although impotence may well be associated with infertility, it must be emphasized that a man might easily be infertile and never have any problems of impotence. Infertile men and women may well enjoy a satisfactory sex life without conception taking place. Sadly there are still those who mistakenly think that if a man cannot father a child he is probably impotent, and in some way 'less than a man'. This is usually completely wrong: many potent men with highly active sex lives are surprised to discover that they may well have been infertile for many years. Infertility had in no way hindered their sexual activity.

Unfortunately, such misguided associations between impotence and infertility may well give the couple who have difficulty in conceiving, immediate feelings of inferiority and guilt, which frequently discourage the man, at least, from seeking advice and reassurance (see page 48). It cannot be emphasized too strongly that whereas impotence may be a problem for a few infertile couples, the vast majority of those seeking advice from doctors have perfectly normal and satisfying sexual relationships.

Defining terms

'Fertility', 'subfertility' and 'infertility' are rather imprecise terms to describe the variation from couples who conceive quickly and easily, through those who experience difficulties requiring medical assistance, to those who after extensive investigation and treatment, remain childless.

Hospital departments dealing with this subject may well be called 'fertility centres' or 'fertility clinics', 'infertility clinics', or even 'subfertility clinics'. All these terms are relative, and without qualification do not mean a great deal.

When to seek advice

It is difficult to say precisely when you should seek advice if you are having difficulty in conceiving a child. There are no strict rules, but most doctors agree that you should not start worrying about your inability to conceive a child until you have been having intercourse without the use of contraceptives for at least 12 to 18 months. However, it is not difficult to see that if, for instance, a woman aged around 35 or more wishes to have a baby, then she and her partner should perhaps try for only a year before seeking advice. On the whole it is better to talk to your doctor earlier rather than later, and if you come forward too soon the doctor can always advise a further spell of trying before beginning investigations.

Health and fertility

Couples who wish to start a family should try to be as healthy as possible at the time of conception. Both partners should avoid being overweight, as obesity in pregnancy can cause a variety of problems. However, avoid becoming too thin as well – this can affect fertility if taken to extremes (see page 33).

Both of you should avoid excessive intakes of alcohol and if at all possible give up smoking. Alcohol and cigarettes both have an adverse affect, especially on male fertility; also, if a pregnancy is achieved, both these powerful drugs (for this is what they are) cross the placenta and may affect a longed-for baby. In fact, a woman should avoid taking drugs of any kind at the time of conception and during pregnancy unless advised to do so by your doctor.

Exercise on a regular basis is a helpful component of healthy living, but excessively hard exercise again may affect fertility. In particular, ovulation may be suppressed in women who work exceptionally hard at athletic pursuits. Again, if in any doubt, consult your doctor.

TWO

Sex and subfertility

It is surprising just how many couples who have difficulty in conceiving are actually perfectly fertile but are experiencing 'technical' problems with sex. Whether they relate to specific sexual difficulties or the timing of intercourse, these problems are very often easily rectified and for obvious reasons the investigating doctor will want to eliminate them before proceeding on to more complicated tests relating to your fertility.

By this time, your doctor will have established that you have spent a reasonable time trying to produce a child before coming forward for help. The next thing he or she will want to do is to make sure that both partners appreciate the normal requirements for fertilization and conception. A very small but ever-present proportion of apparently infertile couples can have their problem solved by a simple explanation of normal requirements. At the very extreme end of this group are couples who are not having normal sexual intercourse – with true failure of technique. Such cases are relatively rare; it is much more common to find that couples have not appreciated the importance of having intercourse reasonably frequently and at the right time in the woman's menstrual cycle.

Frequency of intercourse
Quite obviously, if a couple are having very infrequent intercourse then the chances of conception remain low. Very occasionally, couples will seek help from their doctor and when

The reproductive organs

Male anatomy

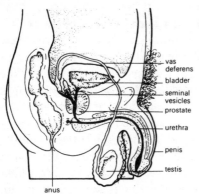

vas deferens
bladder
seminal vesicles
prostate
urethra
penis
testis
anus

Spermatazoon

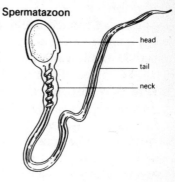

head
tail
neck

Female anatomy

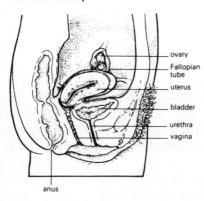

ovary
Fallopian tube
uterus
bladder
urethra
vagina
anus

Ovum

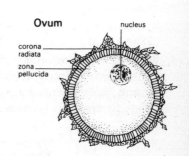

nucleus
corona radiata
zona pellucida

asked will reveal that intercourse may take place perhaps once a month or even less frequently. Work schedules in particular can often interfere with the frequency of intercourse, with one or other partner being out of town, abroad, or working night shifts, for long periods. No one can lay down rules for the frequency of intercourse beyond certain loose guidelines, but many couples can achieve conception simply by changing their schedule to allow more sex at the most advantageous time.

In the course of asking about frequency of intercourse, the doctor may discover that immediately after sex the woman performs vigorous vaginal douching. This practice, which is becoming rarer these days, may well reduce the chances of conception. The reasons behind it may go beyond simple vaginal hygiene; tactful questioning may shed light on the woman's attitude to sex in general, occasionally revealing that she equates the sex act with something that is generally unclean. Further questioning may disclose some strain in the couple's sexual relationship which in itself may have a bearing on the inability to conceive.

It may appear from this that something of a cross-examination is going on, but this is not the case at all. A good doctor is sensitive to the fact that answering intimate questions about one's sex life does not come easily to most people, and he or she will not conduct the interview in the manner of an interrogation. If you feel uncomfortable at the thought of talking about your sex life, remember that the doctor asks such questions only insofar as they are relevant to the job of solving your problem. If serious technical or psycho-sexual difficulties do seem to be occurring, then your doctor may well suggest special counselling from a sex therapist which could benefit both partners.

Timing of intercourse
Even if intercourse is reasonably frequent, it must take place at the time of the month when the woman is most likely to

conceive. This is a matter of only a day or two. We do not know for sure how long *spermatazoa* (sperm) remain viable (able to fertilize the female egg), but a round figure of between 24 and 48 hours seems reasonable. The life of the *ovum* (egg cell) is also relatively short – perhaps only 10 to 12 hours, or sometimes up to 24 hours. It therefore follows that for conception to occur, intercourse must take place within a day or so of ovulation – the moment when the ovum is released from the ovary.

How normal conception works

After a woman has had her menstrual period, the pituitary gland in the brain secretes hormones which stimulate the ripening of an ovum in one of her ovaries (they usually alternate each month). Under the influence of these hormones, the ripe ovum will be released by the ovary. This occurs at approximately the midpoint of the menstrual cycle, although the timing varies, depending on the length of each woman's period (see page 21).

The ovaries are situated close to the *uterus* (womb) near the end of the Fallopian tubes, which lead into the top of the uterus at each side. At the end of the Fallopian tubes are finger-like projections known as *fimbriae* which play over the surface of the ovary. After its release, the ovum is grasped gently by the fimbriae and conducted into the Fallopian tube; it passes down the narrow bore of the tube towards the uterus. During normal sexual intercourse a large number of spermatazoa in the male *ejaculate* (semen) are deposited high inside the vagina, adjacent to the *cervix* (neck of the womb). There can be as many as 500 million sperm. These pass through the plug of mucus situated at the entrance to the womb, in the cervix.

During this passage, the sperm are cleansed of certain proteins and the fluid in which they have travelled. This change is part of an essential process known as *capacitation*, which helps sperm to penetrate the ovum when they meet it in the Fallopian tube. Through uterine contractions the sperm are conducted to the top of the uterus and make their way along the Fallopian tube towards the ovum. Sperm cluster round the ovum, and fertilization occurs when one sperm (and one only) penetrates the ovum. After fertilization, no other sperm is able to enter the ovum.

The ovum and sperm are both single cells which fuse at fertilization. The fertilized ovum remains in the tube and begins to divide, first into two cells, then four, then eight, then sixteen and so on. This process takes about three days, after which the little bundle of cells, looking rather like a mulberry, (hence its medical name of *morula*, Latin for mulberry), migrates down the tube into the uterus. The little mass of cells becomes pressed against its outer membrane, leaving a fluid-filled space. At this stage of development it becomes known as a *blastocyst*. The blastocyst begins to implant itself into the *endometrium* (the glandular lining of the uterus) on the sixth or seventh day after ovulation. The most usual position is at the top and back of the uterus, although it may implant in other parts.

After the release of the ovum from the ovary at the midpoint of the menstrual cycle, the lining of the uterus becomes ready to accept a fertilized ovum. Stimulated by hormones from the ovary, it becomes thickened and more glandular. It also produces nourishing secretions without which the little embryo cannot survive. This second half of the menstrual cycle is frequently referred to as the secretory phase. As the pregnancy progresses and the embryo and its membrane enlarge, further hormones to sustain these processes are produced by the follicle within the ovary from which the ovum was released; the follicle has expanded and while it secretes these hormones, it is known as the *corpus luteum* (yellow body).

If intercourse has not taken place during the day, or within a day or two, or ovulation, or if the ovum is not fertilized, then the enriched lining of the uterus is shed during the menstrual period, triggered by the lowering of hormone levels. After this the whole process starts again.

The best time for sex

It is clear from the above description that the whole process leading to conception depends on the timing of intercourse. Obviously there are numerous other factors which must be fulfilled, but intercourse must take place on or around the time the ovum is released, otherwise viable sperm will not meet a viable ovum in the Fallopian tube. If you are keen to take advantage of this crucial timing to try to achieve conception, then it is generally recommended that the man should abstain from intercourse and masturbation for two or three days beforehand to maximize the number of sperm in his ejaculate before you have intercourse at the mid-cycle time. Most women ovulate on about day 12 to 14 of the cycle. This means that, counting the first day of proper bleeding in the woman's menstruation as day 1 of the cycle, a period of abstinence should be exercised from say, day 6 or 7, with intercourse taking place on day 10 and after a gap of about 48 hours, again on day 12, and maybe on day 14 or 15.

This is only very general advice based on a regular menstrual cycle of 28 days. It must be remembered that the length of the menstrual cycle varies from one woman to another and may also vary in the same woman from month to month. It may be only a day or two's difference, but in some cases up to a week or more, which can make the timing of ovulation difficult to calculate. Besides, many couples would find it awkward and possibly unnatural to have intercourse on a timetable as rigid as an airline flight schedule. However, while the above description is only a rough guide, it is obvious that couples having intercourse only at the beginning or end of the menstrual cycle are unlikely to conceive. (The timing of intercourse and the use of temperature charts is discussed in detail on pages 43–5.)

Most other mammals do not have this timing problem. Dogs and horses, for example, mate only at the time the female is likely to conceive. In other species, such as cats, rabbits and ferrets, the female does not produce an ovum until the

Menstrual cycle

1 Pituitary gland hormones (LH and FSH) stimulate the growth of an egg follicle in the ovary.

2 As the follicle ripens (A), the ovaries produce the hormones progesterone and oestrogen, which stimulate the growth of the lining of the uterus (endometrium). At ovulation (B), the egg (ovum) bursts out of the follicle, is collected by the fimbriae and passes into the fallopian tube.
The empty follicle closes and becomes a corpus luteum (C), producing oestrogen and rising amounts of progesterone. Unless pregnancy occurs, it gradually degenerates.

3 In preparation for receiving an ovum, the endometrium thickens in the first half of the cycle (a). In the second half, (b) glands secrete a rich nutritive substance.

4 Under the influence of ovarian and pituitary hormones, changes also occur in the cervix, vagina

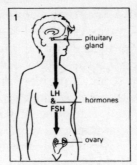

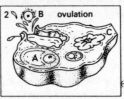

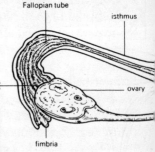

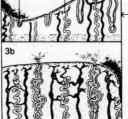

The reproductive cycle

The process by which a woman's body prepares itself for fertilization and pregnancy is complex. However a clear understanding of the mechanisms involved is vital for those seeking treatment for infertility.

and fallopian tubes. The actual release of the ovum is stimulated by a surge of LH (luteinizing hormone) from the pituitary gland. NB The illustration (right) is approximately life size.

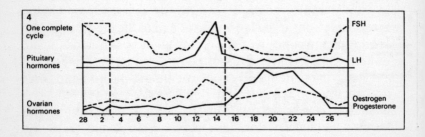

Fertilization and implantation

5 During normal sexual intercourse, several million sperm are deposited high inside the vagina, leaving a pool of semen near the cervix.

6 The sperm travel up into the uterus and then to the fallopian tubes. An ovum will be waiting there if ovulation has occurred.

7 For fertilization to occur, one spermatozoon must enter the ovum (a). Afterwards, the ovum begins to divide into a 2-cell stage (b), then 4, 8, 16 and so on. After about 3 days the ovum, now called a blastocyst (c), reaches the uterus, where it remains free for several days (d).

About 7 days after fertilization, the blastocyst implants into the thickened, glandular endometrium (e), obtaining nutrients from it until the placenta takes over.

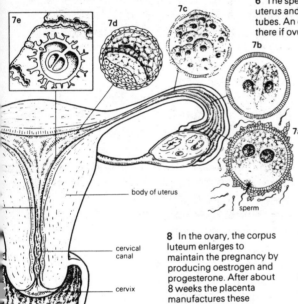

body of uterus

cervical canal

cervix

vagina

sperm

8 In the ovary, the corpus luteum enlarges to maintain the pregnancy by producing oestrogen and progesterone. After about 8 weeks the placenta manufactures these hormones.

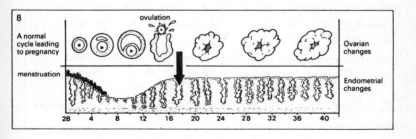

	ovulation						
A normal cycle leading to pregnancy							Ovarian changes
menstruation							Endometrial changes
28	4	8	12	16	20	24	28	32	36	40

spermatazoa have arrived safely in the uterus, while in others, females actually store the sperm successfully until the ovum has been released. Interestingly, however, there is some evidence that women can produce ova at other times than the midcycle, often following emotional or other stimuli. It is not uncommon for couples who practice the 'safe period' as a means of contraception (avoiding intercourse during mid-cycle) to be surprised by a pregnancy ensuing, and this can only be explained by ovulation occurring much earlier or later than expected.

Positions for intercourse

You may wonder whether any particular position during intercourse is more likely to result in pregnancy. While the general answer is no, it is important for the seminal fluid to be deposited near the cervix, and a position which allows a reasonable degree of penetration of the penis into the vagina is therefore desirable. The size of a man's penis is generally unimportant, again so long as penetration is achieved. The vagina is an elastic muscular sheath which can expand to accommodate different-sized male organs.

It is sometimes recommended that a woman should lie on her back for some minutes after sex, perhaps with a cushion underneath her buttocks to allow the sperm to collect near the cervix. On the other hand, some women whose wombs are angled backwards rather than forwards, known as *retroversion* (see page 97), experience discomfort when lying on their backs during intercourse. This may be relieved if the man lies on his back with the woman on top, allowing the uterus to flop forwards out of the way of the penis.

Perhaps the most important aspect of different positions is that by creating variety they enhance enjoyment of sex; in this way they can contribute to a happy sexual relationship, which is beneficial to you both in creating an environment suitable for conception.

24

Contrary to some people's belief, it is not necessary for a woman to have an orgasm for conception to take place. However, an unfulfilled, unsatisfactory sex life may well create stress and tension within the partnership, which, as I have already explained, often appears to inhibit fertility. Furthermore, it is not always necessary for the semen to be deposited at the cervix, and many accidental pregnancies have resulted from the emission of semen at the *vulva* (entrance of the vagina), often after using that most unreliable form of contraception known as the 'withdrawal method' (withdrawal of the penis just before ejaculation).

In general, however, the vagina is hostile to sperm, being too acid for their prolonged survival (they are happiest in a slightly alkaline medium). Consequently, it is far better that the semen is deposited at the cervix as this reduces both the exposure of the sperm to acid vaginal secretions and the distance they have to travel before entering the uterus.

Premature ejaculation

The importance of depositing semen high in the vagina leads us on to what is probably the most common 'technical failure' during sex – premature ejaculation. In this situation, sexual excitement on the part of the man is so intense that ejaculation takes place before the penis is sufficiently deep inside the vagina to ensure depositing the semen close to the cervix. (This condition must not be confused with impotence, which is an inability in the man to produce and maintain an erection, and which is covered later in this chapter.)

Premature ejaculation does not always lead to infertility by any means, and it is remarkable how sperm can sometimes find their way along the length of the vagina to the uterus after having been deposited completely outside the vagina. Premature ejaculation may simply be due to inexperience, but can occur in response to emotional stress or conflict between partners, and men who suffer from this problem may benefit greatly from the advice of a sex therapist. This requires the co-operation of both partners as a woman can be taught to help her partner with this problem which, together with her sympathy and understanding, very often contribute greatly to its solution.

Impotence

Men who are impotent do not usually wait for infertility investigations before seeking help from doctors. There are many different causes of impotence, ranging from physical injury, damage to the nerves which control erection by injury or disease, through ageing to certain drug therapies. However, in a very large proportion of men the condition is the result of mental and emotional disturbance.

A proportion of men who are impotent due to physical causes may respond to treatment: for example, if impotence is a side effect of some form of drug treatment, withdrawal of the drug will cure the condition. However, most physical causes are usually more serious, such as severe nervous diseases or paralysis, and so are incurable.

Men whose impotence is due to severe psychological problems need skilled assistance from psychiatrists and psychotherapists, but the outlook is usually good once the emotional and mental barriers have been breached.

Impotence can also be a transient and less serious problem; many men experience occasional periods of psychologically induced impotence. These often occur during bouts of severe depression and at times of emotional self-assessment and readjustment, particularly in mid-life, which have been described by some as the 'male menopause'. As with premature ejaculation, impotence sometimes appears to be caused by emotional stress between the partners, and in such cases the sympathetic understanding of the woman, perhaps together with the help of a sex therapist, may be all that is necessary to rectify the situation.

For those with true long-standing and incurable impotence, there are devices which enable a man to simulate an erection. As far as fertility is concerned, the big question is whether these devices allow a man to achieve ejaculation and thus father a child. The answer is that it depends on the condition of the appropriate part of the nervous system. Erection is controlled by a chain of nerves in the parasympathetic nervous system, while ejaculation occurs through the action of nerves in the separate sympathetic nervous system. The latter gets the body ready for 'flight, fright and fight' – the blood is diverted from the stomach to the muscles of the legs and arms, the pupils of the eyes dilate, the heart and lungs speed up and sweating occurs. The parasympathetic system causes virtually the reverse action. Thus, even if erection is impaired it may still be possible for the man to ejaculate providing that the relevant part of the nervous system is intact. Young men who are impotent following an injury, for example, may well be able to ejaculate with a mechanical aid to erection in place. However, even when prostheses are used and the nervous system intact, it is important not to underestimate the effects of the powerful psychological forces arising from the malfunction or disease, as these may still inhibit ejaculation.

Painful intercourse

Sometimes infrequent intercourse, and a consequent delay in conceiving, is caused by reluctance on the part of the woman. Worried by this, and perhaps not knowing where to turn for advice, such a woman may well find herself consulting her doctor because she fears 'infertility'. When the doctor comes to the routine questions about frequency of intercourse, and the woman admits that it isn't often, the doctor will question her further as to why and in many cases it is because she doesn't enjoy sex for reasons of pain or fear, or both. An inability to relax the vaginal muscles (vaginal spasm or *vaginismus*) can prevent penetration by the man, turning the sex act into an ordeal at best and a fiasco at worst. Intercourse can become a distressing fight rather than an expression of mutual love: this is obviously not at all conducive to fertility.

Many women who have psychological barriers to intercourse may find it difficult to admit to their partners, their doctors or even to themselves that their problem is one of mental conditioning, and they often complain of pain during intercourse as an expression of their fears and misgivings. When the doctor finds no obvious cause for pain during intercourse, he or she will probably ask tactful questions to seek a psychological cause. If this happens to you, try to answer frankly in the knowledge that all consultations are in the strictest confidence. The outlook for the majority of women in this situation is extremely good – nearly everyone builds up considerable prejudices and fears based on parental attitudes, schooltime myths and early sexual encounters, but these are soon lost in the light of better information and experience.

Women who have such problems need careful counselling to help overcome their fear, and they will also need sympathy and gentle handling from their partners. The use of vaginal dilators is frequently very helpful. Occasionally the doctor will find that the *hymen* (maidenhead) is still intact. The hymen is a thin membrane which partially or completely covers the entrance to the vagina until a woman's first experience of sexual intercourse, or often before if tampons have been used during menstruation. If the hymen is unusually rigid, however, it may prevent entry of the penis. Similarly the doctor may find an unusually small vaginal entrance. The hymen can easily be removed by a small operation, and minor plastic surgery can open up the vaginal entrance.

Vaginal spasm may be the result of a strict upbringing and indicate inhibition about sex, even within marriage. Support, reassurance and advice and the patient understanding of the woman's partner are essential. Sometimes a good meal, wine, soft lights and music can induce the necessary relaxation.

Painful intercourse can also have physical causes, which are often also associated with infertility. Internal or external infection may have something to do with it, and this will be treated before further investigations. A retroverted uterus may also cause a certain amount of pain on deep penetration as has already been mentioned, but the most common physical cause of pain, and one which is in itself a cause of infertility, is *endometriosis*. This condition and its treatment are discussed at length later, on page 65.

THREE

Preliminary investigations

Once it has been established that you have been trying for a baby for at least a year without success, and that there are no technical problems with sex, then you will start preliminary investigations into the possible causes of your inability to conceive. Your general practitioner may already have referred you to a specialist clinic or he or she may have made the initial tactful enquiries about any technical problems with sex. Either way, the next step will almost certainly take place together in a specialist clinic. Facing up to problems with fertility is hard for both partners, but its treatment must be a shared endeavour. There are many reasons for subfertility or infertility, in both men and women, and they have to be systematically investigated.

Routine questions for the woman

Investigations usually start with the woman. At your first consultation, your doctor will be looking initially for any immediate clue to the cause of the problem. Much can be gleaned in a few minutes of sensible questioning and you should not feel embarrassed or resentful at being asked a great number of questions, the immediate relevance of which may not always be apparent. As in all investigations, much time-wasting effort and inconvenience can be caused by missing an important piece of information that could have been produced during the routine questioning at the beginning. The experienced doctor will quickly assess your answers and home in on those pieces of information which appear to be most relevant.

Family and medical history
Infertility cannot be said to be inherited. However, family history can be significant, and it may be relevant to know, for instance, if any close relatives suffer from diabetes, or that one of your parents died of tuberculosis. More important, though, is your own previous medical history, so you should expect to relate all the medical problems you may have had in the past. Serious illnesses, venereal diseases and operations may all be relevant, and also any previous pregnancies and whether they ended in normal birth, miscarriage or termination of pregnancy.

For instance, the venereal disease gonorrhoea may cause infection to spread into the Fallopian tubes, causing blockage or damage to their delicate linings. Operations in the area of the pelvis, such as appendectomy, may cause infection or *adhesions* (the formation of scar tissue) around the tubes and ovaries, with adverse results. Evidence of previous pregnancies can help to show the doctor whether there has been potential for conception – if a woman has managed to conceive a child in the past, even if it did not result in a live birth, what has happened subsequently to prevent her conceiving again?

In fact, any operations on the gynaecological organs – uterus, Fallopian tubes, ovaries, vagina, vulva – must be recorded. It may be that you are unsure of the exact details of such operations and may possibly be embarrassed to describe your symptoms and ideas about the surgery. However, your doctor can always check the records of the hospital concerned to find out the exact surgical details of what took place. A typical case may be if you had an operation to remove an *ectopic* pregnancy (where the embryo starts to develop outside the uterus, most frequently in a Fallopian tube); in the days of upset, discomfort and anxiety that followed you may have become confused as to whether the surgeon removed part or all of the tube, even though it may have been explained to you at the time.

Menstrual history

The doctor will of course take a detailed menstrual history. The age at which your periods first started (known as the *menarche*) is recorded as well. Most girls start to menstruate between 11 and 14, although variations on either side are quite common. The first few periods tend to be painless and ovulation does not take place; when ova are produced with each cycle then the periods tend to produce cramping pain to a greater or lesser degree. The age at which the menarche occurs is getting earlier and earlier in well-nourished societies and the menopause (when periods stop) later and later – thus the span of a woman's fertility is gradually being extended. In underdeveloped countries this span is reduced and the menarche comes later. In Shakespeare's time the onset of a girl's periods occurred much later than it does in the healthier and better nourished days of this century: nowadays in Western countries 95 per cent of girls with normal ovulation will have menstruated by the age of sixteen.

A delay in the onset of periods may indicate that the ovaries are not functioning correctly. A complete absence of pain with periods and an irregular menstrual cycle may also suggest a failure or impairment of ovulation. No menstrual bleeding for months, or even years (*amenorrhoea*) may also suggest that the ovaries are not functioning properly or that there is some deficiency in the chain of hormones which activate the menstrual cycle.

The same goes for scanty or irregular periods. It should be said straight away that sudden changes of surroundings or occupation, excessive worry, tension caused by examinations or emotional problems, and marked weight loss, may all cause temporary amenorrhoea which frequently ceases when surroundings, activities or weight return to normal. The classic cases of this are girls who go away to college or to work abroad. When periods stop, fear that they might be pregnant adds to their worries. However, women in this situation are not likely to come along to their doctor complaining of infertility; on the contrary, they are usually relieved to find out they are not pregnant right in the middle of their first term at college!

Women who suffer a marked drop in weight and cease to menstruate do tend to seek medical help because they are not likely to conceive; usually the problem is manifested at the first interview with a sensible doctor. Going on a weight-gaining diet is usually all that is required for periods to resume. We don't know the exact mechanism by which periods stop when weight drops, but periods, fertility and nutrition are all closely interrelated. A very restrictive diet may reduce your body weight to what it was before the menarche, or to a level at which you would not have the reserves of strength to support a pregnancy, and so it is understandable that the ovaries are 'switched off'. This is an over-simplification of the situation, of course. However, we do know that weight-related amenorrhoea, as well as the effects of emotions and instinctive drives such as hate, rage, love and hunger, are controlled in some way by the hypothalamus – an area at the base of the brain just above the pituitary gland, which it also controls. Physiologists still have much to discover about how this small but immensely important part of our brain works.

The effect of contraceptives

Another factor to be considered is the method of contraception you have been using in the past, if any. The barrier methods (the sheath or condom and the diaphragm) are not likely to have any effect on fertility after their use is stopped. Oral contraceptives (the pill) and the intra-uterine contraceptive device (IUCD or the coil) – can cause occasional problems.

33

Women who use oral contraceptives are often worried that they may have difficulty in becoming pregnant when they want to have a child, especially if they have been taking the pill for a considerable time. Happily, most women who stop taking the pill do not have to wait very long before becoming pregnant, and when problems do occur (that is, if a woman does not begin to ovulate again and have normal periods), effective medical treatment is available. The reason why women are anxious about the effects of the pill is usually that they are aware that, by taking it, they are interfering with the usual hormone levels in their bodies. While this is a very understandable worry, it might reassure people to know more about how the pill works; now that the oral contraceptive has been in use for nearly 30 years, our knowledge of it is considerable.

The most common type of pill contains synthetic oestrogen and progestogen hormones, and its main action is to prevent ovulation. The synthetic hormones are very similar to those that circulate in the body at raised levels during pregnancy, and the body responds to their presence in the same way, by switching off the ovulation mechanism.

As soon as you stop taking the pill, hormone levels fall and a 'withdrawal' bleed occurs; when the pill is taken cyclically for three weeks out of every four, a normal menstrual period is simulated with a withdrawal bleed occurring in the fourth week. If before starting the pill you were ovulating normally and experienced regular satisfactory periods, it is likely that your normal periods will return immediately you stop taking the pill, particularly if you have been taking one of the modern low-dose preparations.

However, a small number of women do experience 'post-pill amenorrhoea'; in these cases periods are usually 'switched on' again with one of the fertility drugs (see page 86). Today the problem occurs much less frequently than a few years ago. In the early days, oral contraceptives were used by some practitioners to 'regularize' very irregular periods in some women. We now know that those women were probably not ovulating regularly, or at all, and in some cases the injudicious use of oral contraceptives may have had the effect of suppressing ovulation and the menstrual cycle after the pill was discontinued.

Nowadays, doctors are not happy to prescribe the pill unless satisfied that your menstrual cycle has been normal and regular, suggesting normal ovulation, for at least a year. If not, he or she would suggest some other form of contraception which does not run the risk of suppressing an already scanty pattern of ovulation.

Fertility and the coil

The effect of the intra-uterine contraceptive device, or coil as it is commonly called, on subsequent fertility is a frequently raised question to which, again, there is no clear-cut answer. Women who have a coil fitted do not usually have any problems in conceiving when it is taken out. Provided that the modern type of IUCD now in use is fitted properly and checked by a doctor experienced in family planning, the risk to subsequent fertility is minimal. However, there have been recent suggestions that IUCDs fitted to women who have not had a child may set up a low-grade inflammation in the lining of the uterus which may not cause any symptoms of pain or fever, but which could delay subsequent fertility when the IUCD is removed. Because of this, some doctors do not advise use of an IUCD by a childless woman without extensive discussion.

Previous pregnancies or miscarriages

Quite a few women seeking help for infertility will have been pregnant in the past. Obviously, if you have had a child, or even a pregnancy which ended in a miscarriage or termination you have demonstrated that you have or at least have had the ability to produce children – whereas this is not the case with a woman with primary infertility. The doctor will therefore record full details of any previous pregnancies and, significantly, who fathered them. A woman whose second marriage is barren after she had children by her first husband is bound to suspect that her second husband is infertile. However, as this is by no means always the case, a wise doctor will be slow to jump to any conclusions without proper investigations.

Details of deliveries of children in the past are important. Infections after childbirth may in a few unfortunate women result in subsequent infertility. Any findings reported by the surgeon at a Caesarean section may also be relevant, and subsequent infection would also be of interest.

In many cases, of course, pregnancies may have occurred in the past but not reached full term: if you have had a miscarriage it can be an encouraging sign in that it indicates the apparatus for conception is functioning to some extent at least. The Hollywood cliché of the woman who has a miscarriage and then is unable to conceive ever again is, in fact, extremely rare. Miscarriage is much more common than people realize: one in five pregnancies ends in miscarriage (see page 80). A straight-forward miscarriage in the first twelve weeks of pregnancy with no problems afterwards will not cause sterility. Infection of the uterus or Fallopian tubes, however, might cause infertility in some cases.

Termination of pregnancy (*therapeutic abortion*) may damage the reproductive organs if it is not performed under sterile conditions. Even a termination performed in approved hospitals and clinics is occasionally followed by infection and/ or damage to the uterus or Fallopian tubes. However, since the woman is under competent medical supervision, these complications are usually treated swiftly and the chances of subsequent infertility are considerably reduced (see page 79).

Breastfeeding

Nature, of course, produces its own period of infertility after the birth of a baby. During breastfeeding most women do not menstruate and are unlikely to become pregnant. However, about one-third of women will ovulate *before* weaning is completed and are therefore fertile, even if they haven't menstruated yet. Most doctors suggest the use of contraceptives during breastfeeding unless you want to become pregnant again quite quickly. However, if you are seeking advice about infertility following childbirth, remember that it is normal for breastfeeding to prevent ovulation and therefore conception.

The physical examination

After taking your medical history, it is usual for your doctor to give you a physical examination. With the advent of complex biochemical tests that can be performed in the laboratory and the increasing use of medical technology, especially ultrasound scanning, the importance of the physical examination is declining in infertility work, as it is to some extent in all fields of medicine. Nowadays the cause of most cases of infertility in women could be discovered with a few blood tests and a *laparoscopy* (see page 72). However, in case the cause of the infertility is one of the more obscure varieties, most doctors still prefer to give a careful physical examination at the beginning of infertility investigations. This is because a doctor's examination can provide clues which will put the succession of blood tests, x-rays, etc, on the right track and occasionally cut out unnecessary procedures.

The examination can be divided into two parts – a general examination of your whole body, and the internal pelvic examination, which specifically allows the doctor to feel the state of your reproductive organs with his or her hands. The doctor will first of all get an overall impression of your weight-to-height ratio and your physical and sexual development.

External checks

Your thyroid gland will be felt with the fingertips, a procedure known as *palpating*. The gland lies in the neck, just in front of the windpipe, and is shield-like in appearance (which is what the word 'thyroid' means). It controls the general level of metabolism, the rate at which the body 'ticks over'. Increased activity of the thyroid gland speeds up the pulse rate, makes a person feel warm even when others feel cold, burns up a good deal of extra energy – and tends to shorten or abolish menstrual periods. Decreased activity of the thyroid slows the body down in several ways and may prolong menstrual periods and make them heavy (*menorrhagia*). Both states may affect fertility. Such malfunction of the thyroid may sometimes be felt by the doctor as an enlargement of the whole gland or one of its lobes.

When you are examined, you may be puzzled to find the doctor looking into your eyes with a small lighted instrument, known as an ophthalmoscope. Although the condition that he or she is checking for is relatively uncommon, all doctors will want to rule it out. In a few instances, infertility may be due to abnormalities in the brain. A small tumour in the pituitary gland in the base of the brain can interfere with normal hormone production and might occasionally account for infertility in an otherwise healthy woman. It could also cause the pituitary gland to enlarge and press on the nerves leading from the retina at the back of the eyes to the brain. This can cause changes in the area where the nerves reach the back of the eye which are sometimes visible on inspecting the retina with an ophthalmoscope.

Your blood pressure will be checked and your abdomen examined briefly – any operation scars will be noted, in case in the heat of the moment you have forgotten to mention abdominal surgery. It is not uncommon for a doctor to ask, 'Any serious operations in the past?' and receive the reply 'No,' only to find an appendicectomy scar during the physical examination!

Internal checks
Last of all comes the pelvic examination. Unfortunately, the

thought of this fills some women with anxiety and apprehension, especially if they have not been examined before. Sometimes this anxiety tends to cloud the medical history-taking and preliminary chat with the doctor, and several important questions might not be fully taken in.

Let me say at the outset that the internal pelvic examination should be nothing worse than uncomfortable; in the majority of cases it is completely painless. Occasionally, there might be slight pain when, for example, the doctor discovers there is tenderness of the ovaries and Fallopian tubes and then tries further to assess the degree of tenderness; but in the normal healthy woman a pelvic examination conducted in a relaxed and professional atmosphere should not hurt at all. Any doctor who does hurt a woman during a routine examination should be rebuked by the person in no uncertain terms. A rigorous, painful examination is likely to undermine any confidence and trust between the couple and the doctor carrying out the investigations.

In the pelvic examination, the organs are felt through layers of skin, fat and muscle, and minor abnormalities can be difficult to detect. Of much more use are the techniques of direct vision allowed by the laparoscope, but these do require a stay in hospital and the use of a general anaesthetic. (This comes much later in the investigations: see page 72.) But the value of the pelvic examination lies in the fact that obvious problems, such as active pelvic inflammatory disease or major abnormalities of the reproductive organs can be detected or ruled out as early as possible.

If you haven't had one recently, the doctor may suggest taking a cervical smear for testing. While the speculum is in position for the smear, the doctor will also have a good look at the state of the cervix and the part of the vagina visible. Particular note will be taken of any vaginal discharge which might benefit from treatment, but is probably not a cause of infertility. More important is the state of the cervix itself.

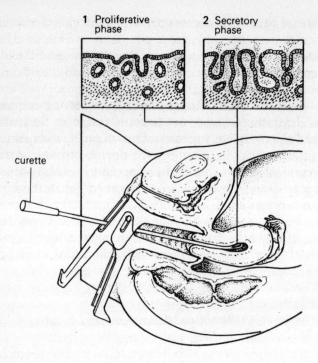

Performing an endometrial biopsy. A small sample of cells from the lining of the womb is scraped off during the second half of the menstrual cycle (secretory phase). This can indicate whether ovulation is occurring.

Reduced fertility can sometimes be due to chronic infections of the cervix (*cervicitis*) since this produces a hostile environment which is usually too acid for sperm and perhaps does not allow capacitation to take place. (Incidentally, when doctors say 'chronic' they mean 'longstanding', and when they say 'acute' they mean 'of quick onset' or 'of short duration'. The terms relate only to time and not to severity. It is incorrect to say 'the pain was very acute' when you mean the pain was severe – an acute pain is one which comes on quickly.)

On rare occasions, doctors perform a test called *endometrial biopsy* during the physical examination. This consists of removing a small piece of tissue from the lining of the uterus, the endometrium. By introducing a small rod into the uterus through the cervical canal a tiny sample can be scraped out and sent for examination. Its appearance under the microscope helps determine whether ovulation is occurring and whether the endometrium has become receptive to allow implantation and growth of the fertilized egg. This procedure can be painful to a varying degree, so is more often done during laparoscopy (see page 76) when you are under a general anaesthetic.

The last procedure is the bimanual internal pelvic examination. For this, you lie on your back with your knees flopped apart. The doctor, wearing a lubricated glove, inserts first and second fingers into the vagina while the other hand presses

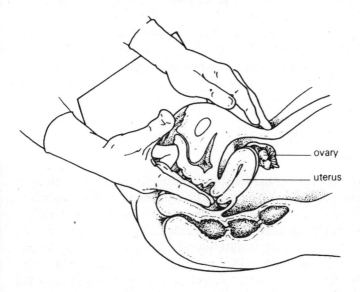

ovary
uterus

The technique of bimanual examination. The doctor can feel the size and shape of the uterus, and its mobility.

down on your lower abdomen. The doctor is feeling the size and shape of your uterus which, if abnormal, may be a sign of problems associated with infertility. For instance, a knobbly uneven uterus would suggest the presence of fibroids, benign swellings in the uterine muscle. A normal womb has a fair degree of mobility, and where the womb is found to be fixed, there is a strong possibility that you have had previous episodes of pelvic inflammatory disease which may have caused blocked Fallopian tubes. A tender, relatively immobile womb might also be due to the condition of *endometriosis* which can also cause infertility (see page 65).

A womb which is badly misshapen by multiple fibroids may not allow satisfactory implantation of the fertilized ovum, and even if this does take place, miscarriage early in the pregnancy may result. The finding of one or two small fibroids – and most women over 30 do have one or more, usually very small – is hardly likely to account for infertility, however.

The ovaries, which are about the size and shape of large almonds, will also be felt. If they are enlarged, they may be *polycystic* – containing numerous small cysts. Thickening of the tubes and ovaries often suggests that there has been inflammation in the past, or, if the tubes and ovaries are tender, that inflammation is more recent or current. In both cases the result may be blockage of the Fallopian tubes.

FOUR

The next steps

The way a doctor plans the course of fertility investigations is open to much variation. One important factor is your age. For example, if a woman aged 38 wishes for infertility investigations and treatment (which could take up to two years) the doctor must get moving quickly. A younger woman who has only been trying for a baby for about a year and who from her history and examination does not appear to have any serious problem might have her investigations in a more leisurely fashion.

Another factor which will help to determine the type and sequence of tests is your medical history. A woman who has not menstruated for a year or more will require different management from one who has no menstrual irregularity and whose problem might be blocked Fallopian tubes. However, all things being equal, most doctors start off by asking the woman to keep temperature charts and by recommending that the man has a *seminalysis*, or sperm test, at this stage.

Both of these are important. Temperature charts offer an easy method of seeing if ovulation is actually taking place: this must be established early on, since about 20 per cent of cases of female infertility are due to ovulatory failure. In addition, because filling in the charts involves a sustained effort on your part, they give an indication of your motivation. If you find you can't really be bothered to keep temperature charts, it might be worth asking yourself just how keen you really are to conceive. This will certainly be going through your doctor's mind if he or she finds you have not been filling in the charts regularly. In this situation the doctor is entitled to wonder whether a woman is attending the clinic because her partner has sent her, or whether both partners genuinely want to proceed with investigations.

The seminalysis, where the man collects a sample of seminal fluid for examination, is equally important, because the results can determine which partner should be investigated first. There is not much point in proceeding with tests and invasive surgical procedures on a woman if the seminalysis shows that her partner is almost certainly infertile. The correct specimen containers and instructions are therefore often provided at this first visit (see page 53).

Temperature charts

If you are given temperature charts, you will be asked to take your temperature daily and record it on the chart for at least a month and probably for three or four months in succession. It is important to do this as soon as you wake up in the morning, that is to say, before you raise your temperature artificially by drinking tea or coffee, or lower it by cleaning your teeth with cold water. In the first half of the cycle your temperature is slightly lower than the second half after ovulation takes place. This is known as a *biphasic* pattern. Typically, just before ovulation there is a little 'kick down' and then at ovulation there is a rise of nearly 0.5° C (1° F), which is sustained until menstruation takes place. If pregnancy occurs you do not menstruate and the temperature remains slightly elevated. You should not, of course, be smoking if you are trying to become pregnant but, if you are, take your temperature before smoking in the mornings.

The charts are started on the first day of menstrual bleeding with a new chart for each period. You will probably also be asked to mark the days on which sexual intercourse took place. If they have been kept properly these charts are extremely useful and provide answers to the following questions:

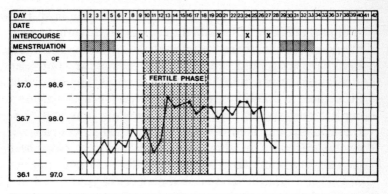

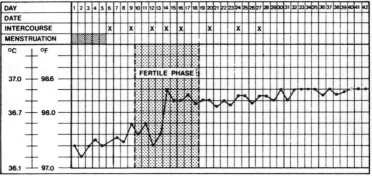

*Typical temperature charts. Top: Normal pattern for ovulation. Above:
Pattern for ovulation and pregnancy, with prolonged elevated temperature.
Little or no elevation would indicate that ovulation has not occurred.*

1 Is the pattern biphasic (does it seem likely that you are
   ovulating)?
2 Are the menstrual periods prolonged, heavy, light, scanty, or
   occasionally absent?
3 When does ovulation appear to occur in relation to the
   periods? (Some women have a longer-than-average cycle and
   ovulate later than the thirteenth or fourteenth day.)
4 Most importantly, is intercourse occurring at the optimum
   time for conception, near to ovulation?

Now, unless your medical history and examination suggest any abnormalities that require immediate investigation, many doctors will leave more complex tests to the second and subsequent visits, and see you again when the completed temperature charts and seminalysis results are available. Unless there is a really urgent need to get on with the more complex tests, your doctor will take the initial investigations rather slowly and methodically, because some couples will conceive early on in the treatment after they have been reassured by the doctor – sometimes after only one visit. So, don't be surprised if that is all that happens at your first visit – history-taking, examination, provision of temperature charts and a specimen container for seminalysis.

Conversely, don't be alarmed if any further tests are ordered at this stage. Doctors vary in their approach, and some may do initial screening such as a chest x-ray, thyroid function tests, etc, as a matter of systematic routine, rather than because they particularly suspect, say, some malfunction of the thyroid gland.

The postcoital test

One test that many doctors like to perform early on in the investigations is a 'postcoital test', particularly just before the second appointment. You will be asked to have sexual intercourse between two and four hours before your appointment and you should not bathe, shower or douche yourself before going to the doctor's clinic, as this may wash the sperm away. The doctor will inspect the cervix with a vaginal speculum (the same type that is used to take a smear) and a small blob of cervical mucus is taken, placed on a slide and examined there and then under a microscope. The test is painless. The doctor will look for the presence of sperm and, if they are present, whether they are moving about freely.

Finding no sperm, along with a low sperm count at seminalysis, would suggest that the man might be infertile and should have further tests; the finding of many dead or vibrating sperm stuck within the mucus might indicate the presence of antisperm antibodies.

Sometimes there is an unusual explanation for the absence of sperm at the postcoital test. On occasion I have met women who have practised vigorous vaginal douching immediately after intercourse; this does not allow time for the sperm to penetrate the cervical mucus and get into the womb. At the postcoital test there was no sign of sperm, not even a trace of semen, yet the results of seminalysis were good. One such woman had been brought up strictly to believe that cleanliness was next to godliness, and she felt that the presence of semen inside her vagina, even for an hour or two, was in some way unclean, so following intercourse she would rush off to the bathroom. I am happy to say that when she stopped this immediate vaginal douching she conceived within two months. This uncommon cause of infertility would not have come to light without the postcoital test, which is a safe, simple but extremely useful procedure.

FIVE

Male Infertility

A certain amount of strain and mistrust can easily arise between a couple who fail to produce a much-wanted baby. It is important for both partners to face the prospects of infertility together and not to apportion blame – either consciously or subconsciously – to the other. It sometimes happens that men are reluctant to come forward for examination, even though they are happy to allow their partners to undergo a lengthy process of investigation. This reluctance may be because the man (mistakenly) associates fertility with virility, or sexual prowess, and is afraid of being found to be infertile.

Initial checks

It is very important that the male partner should be examined as soon as possible, and that he has a *seminalysis* or sperm count. In a considerable proportion of couples who are investigated, a problem is found in the man (estimates vary between 10 and 50 per cent), and because of this doctors are reluctant to put women through the much more invasive tests involved in pinpointing their problems with infertility until they have ruled out problems in their partners.

In most cases the results of the seminalysis will play an important part in determining what further tests should be carried out on both of you. For instance, if the sperm count is not good a man is usually referred to a urologist for specialist help (a urologist is a doctor who specializes in kidney and bladder complaints, and in conditions associated with the male reproductive organs). If, however, the sperm count is good, investigations on his partner will be continued. But if these don't show up a definite cause of infertility then her partner may again be referred for more exhaustive tests despite his seemingly normal sperm count.

Low sperm count

If the results of the seminalysis show you have a moderate to low sperm count you will either be referred to a urologist, as explained before, or treated in the fertility clinic. Further tests can be carried out, including at least two or three additional seminalyses to check whether the impairment is temporary or permanent. Usually, however, doctors will recommend that simple investigations are carried out on your partner at the same time for several reasons. Firstly, many men with low or moderately low sperm counts are quite capable of fathering children, and secondly, there may also be some easily remedied cause of infertility in your partner. She may not be ovulating, for example, which can be rectified with drugs (see page 86). The fact is that on the practical side there is more chance of helping a subfertile woman than a subfertile man, given the present state of knowledge.

The majority of men undergoing further investigation, therefore, will be those whose sperm counts are low and whose partners have already undergone simple investigations and have been found to be normal. In a large proportion of couples where the man attends a male clinic, a pregnancy will be achieved within six months. The success rate has been shown to be over 50 per cent in two separate studies, but this figure may owe more to the reassurance given by the examination than to the efficacy of treatment.

Although most descriptions of male fertility centre on the sperm count, this is by no means an infallible yardstick. It is just not possible to say with certainty that one man has a low sperm count and is therefore infertile, or that another has a high sperm count and is obviously fertile. There are so many exceptions to both rules. But it is important to understand how sperm are formed and function before any discussion of the treatment of male infertility and any difficulties associated with it.

Spermatazoa

Spermatazoa, more usually known as sperm, are tiny tadpole-shaped cells; each has a long whip-like tail which permits it a considerable degree of mobility, and a head full of nuclear protein containing half the number of chromosomes required to construct a person. (The female ovum contains the corresponding number so when they fuse the resulting new cell has the right number of chromosomes to develop into a new person.) Sperm also carry the important X or Y chromosomes which determine the sex of a baby.

Sperm are manufactured in the testes, beginning at puberty and continuing throughout a man's life into old age. The production of sperm is stimulated by a hormone (known as the follicle-stimulating hormone) secreted by the pituitary gland at the base of the brain.

Structure of the testes

The testes each contain a very long, thin tube wound tightly on itself, rather like the elastic inside a golfball; on top of the testes, which are the size of large walnuts, sits a slightly wider tube, again folded on itself, called the *epididymis*. Under the influence of hormones from the pituitary gland, sperm develop in the cells lining the tubes of the testes. When mature they are released into the bore of the tube and pass along to be stored in the epididymis. This is connected to the *vas deferens* – the long muscular tube which sends the sperm on their way to the outside world.

Sperm are conducted by the vas deferens up into the abdominal cavity, along the base of the bladder, and through

Sperm production

- vas deferens
- bladder
- prostate gland
- urethra
- testes
- seminal vesicles

Cross-section of testis

- spermatic cord
- vas deferens
- epididymis
- seminiferous tubule

Spermatazoa are produced in tubules of the testis and stored in the epididymis. Sperm travel up the vasa deferentia and mix with secretions from the seminal vesicles and prostate gland to form the ejaculate.

the prostate gland into the urethra (the small, muscular tube which conducts urine from the bladder through the penis). The sperm then pass through the urethra and out of the penis. While passing under the base of the bladder the sperm and the fluid surrounding them, together known as the *ejaculate*, are joined by a secretion from two glands known as the *seminal vesicles*. Another secretion produced by the prostate gland precedes the ejaculate in its journey from the prostate to the penis.

Undescended testis

The two testes are originally formed early in fetal development in the abdomen, near the kidneys, and as the baby develops they gradually move down, passing through a canal in the groin (the *inguinal canal*) so that at birth they are in the bag of skin known as the *scrotum*. It is thought that the testes are suspended outside the body because they function better at a temperature several degrees lower than that of the rest of the body.

It is not uncommon for one or both of the testes not to descend fully so that at birth they are still within the abdominal cavity – a condition known as undescended testis. Testes which have become lodged in the groin canal can sometimes be brought down into the scrotum by a small operation, usually performed during early childhood. (This is important for if left undescended there is a risk of cancer.) Unfortunately it is not uncommon for a testis which has been successfully brought down to fail to produce spermatazoa. However, one functioning testis is generally sufficient to ensure fertility, and if it is properly descended at birth or soon after, no problem usually arises.

The prostate gland

I must say a brief word about the prostate gland, since few people seem to understand its position within the male apparatus. Scientists are still unsure of all its functions and it is the subject of much research. The prostate gland is a walnut-sized organ which encircles the neck of the bladder like a hand grasping the neck of a bottle. Through it passes the urethra. At the prostate gland the urethra is joined by the two vas deferens from the testes. Thus the male urethra is used not only for the passage of urine but for the passage of sperm as well. Fertility can be impaired by long-term infections of the prostate. Men with such infections have sometimes been successful in making their partners pregnant after a course of suitable antibiotics.

Seminalysis

I have already discussed the need for a seminalysis or sperm count early on in your investigations as a couple (see page 44). This is done by collecting a direct sample following masturbation; collecting after interrupted intercourse is unsatisfactory since the sample may be incomplete, and the first portion of the ejaculate, which contains the most sperm, may be missed. It is not satisfactory to collect a sample in a condom either as most condoms are coated with a substance which is designed to kill sperm.

Instead you will be given a special plastic container in which to collect the sample at your first visit to the clinic, along with printed instructions. You will probably be asked to warm the container to body heat before ejaculation and to keep it at this temperature for at least 15 minutes afterwards. Research has shown that if this is done and cooling is allowed to take place gradually afterwards there is no need for extra warm wrapping during transportation to the laboratory.

It is helpful if you have abstained from masturbation and intercourse for two or three days prior to the collection in order to maximize the number of sperm present. The sample must be delivered to the laboratory within two to four hours of collection, and sooner if possible.

In the laboratory the sample of semen is examined under the microscope. The technician will be looking for at least 20 million sperm per millilitre of fluid (the quantity of ejaculate varies between 2 and 6ml) and preferably much higher, of which 40 per cent or more should be actively *motile* (which means seen to be actively swimming by wriggling their bodies). A further search is made for abnormal cells or sperm with double heads, double tails or short tails. A normal sample should contain less than 30 per cent of these abnormal forms. The size of the individual cells is also assessed, and although it does not matter if all the cells are large, or all small, the presence of sperm cells of different sizes is associated with subfertility. The laboratory technician will also be looking for the presence of other substances, which might indicate infection of some sort.

The results of seminalysis depend on the circumstances in which the collection was made and also on interpretations by the technician performing the analysis. A great many factors will influence the actual number and quality of the sperm in each individual sample. Obviously, if intercourse has been extremely frequent, the count tends to be somewhat lower as the sperm generation cycle can take between six and ten weeks. Counts may also depend on your physical condition and indeed even on the time of day the collection was made. However, these are usually subtle variations rather than abnormalities which may indicate infertility, and anyway further samples are always requested if a man is found to have a low sperm count (*oligospermia*) or no sperm at all (*azoospermia*) to double-check the result.

Seminalysis is open to a great deal of debate, and assessment of male infertility is still bedevilled by the impossibility of defining fertility purely in terms of the sperm count. For instance, the figure of 20 million sperm per ml has been widely regarded as an approximate dividing line between fertility and infertility, but even this figure is subject to doubt. As long ago as 1951 a very large study found that 84 per cent of the husbands in infertile marriages had sperm counts of over 20 million per ml, but many men with counts of less than 20 million had successfully fathered children.

There is also some disagreement about what constitutes an abnormal sperm. In one study, samples of 500 sperm were sent to 47 experts who produced different opinions about half the specimens they looked at! As you can see, this is not an area of medical knowledge in which it is possible to reach absolute conclusions.

Further investigations

In spite of the controversy, if repeated seminalysis shows a persistently low sperm count, you may be referred for further investigations by a male infertility specialist. The first step will be to take a complete medical history, as with your partner. The doctor will be looking for any illnesses or conditions, past or present, which could possibly cause or contribute to infertility, so be ready for a lengthy enquiry.

Medical history

The doctor may begin by asking whether there was any problem in childhood with the descent of the testes into the scrotum and, in particular, whether you had an operation in childhood. The doctor may also ask whether any abdominal operations have been performed, such as a hernia repair; this is because, as in women, the formation of adhesions or the development of infection following an operation can impair fertility. The doctor will also inquire whether you have had mumps, or venereal diseases such as gonorrhoea and syphilis; these infections sometimes produce sterility by destroying the sperm-producing tissue of the testes or blocking the ducts which convey sperm out of the testes.

Environmental factors may also be relevant: for example, living for long periods at high altitudes has been shown to interfere with the production of sperm. Your doctor will also ask whether you have been exposed to radiation or drugs, and whether your occupation involves contact with chemicals or exposure to high temperatures, all of which may have some influence on fertility. General physical condition is also important, as sperm production may be unsatisfactory if a man is an invalid, grossly obese, a heavy drinker and/or smoker. Wearing tight-fitting underpants is thought to raise the scrotal temperature, which has an adverse effect on the sperm.

If no abnormality is discovered, blood tests may be performed to rule out a hormonal cause of the problem, although these often prove to be normal. If so, you may simply be recommended to wear loose-fitting underpants and to apply occasional cold douches to the scrotum. These simple measures are sometimes sufficient to improve the sperm count. The doctor will also inquire whether you believe you have ever made a woman pregnant in the past and if any significant events have taken place since that time to account for the apparent loss of fertility (for instance, a mumps infection). It is important to be frank about answering such questions, which will of course be treated in strict confidence, as they have a direct bearing on possible diagnosis and treatment of impaired fertility.

The physical examination

The second step will be a physical examination. In the majority of men, this reveals no cause of infertility but an explanation will be found in a few cases. Poor body-hair growth or underdeveloped genitals may indicate a hormone deficiency; hormone levels in the blood can then be tested and treatment may be recommended (see page 61). In a very few cases, undescended testes will be found and an operation recommended. This is mainly to avoid the risk of cancer already mentioned.

A far more common physical cause of male infertility is a *varicocele*. This is an abnormality of the blood vessels in the scrotum which become widely dilated and tortuous and show as an enlarged area of the scrotum which feels a bit like a bag of worms. You will be examined standing up when the doctor searches for a possible varicocele.

A varicocele is most commonly seen on the left side of the scrotum. It causes abnormally high blood flow through the scrotum which has the effect of raising the temperature around the testes, and although sperm motility, quality and density may be normal, it is thought that the raised temperature has an important effect on sperm. I should point out that, as with everything to do with male infertility, varicoceles do not behave in a completely predictable fashion, and approximately two-thirds of men who have one are not infertile. However, in those who are thought to be infertile the treatment of a varicocele should be given high priority. A minor operation is performed to tie off or remove the varicocele. The results of such an operation are variable, but it is claimed that more than half the men operated on subsequently succeed in making their partners pregnant.

The course of further investigations

The results of the seminalysis, medical history and the physical examination determine the course of further investigations. If no definite cause of infertility is discovered, you may be offered more complex tests but this depends very much on the facilities available. Whereas in the investigations of female infertility, clear trends in tests and treatment emerge, there are much greater gaps in the understanding of male infertility and methods of treatment are in many cases still experimental. So it is difficult to predict the exact course of any further treatment you may be offered. However, I can describe the various methods available.

Although this is by no means a clear-cut distinction, we can very roughly divide the men who would still be under investigation into two camps: those whose sperm count is low, and those whose sperm count is normal.

Treatment for men with a low sperm count is described on page 61. Where the sperm count is not the critical factor, what needs to be discovered is how the sperm fare inside your partner's body: how they progress from the vagina through the cervix and into the uterus and Fallopian tubes.

The role of cervical mucus

Placing the tip of the penis high up the vagina during intercourse ensures that the ejaculate is deposited at the cervix, on the neck of the womb. The sperm then penetrate a protective plug of mucus which fills the small opening of the cervical canal into the cavity of the uterus. This is a very important process: complex chemical changes, known as *capacitation*, take place as the sperm travel through the mucus and the rest of the female reproductive tract. These changes greatly affect the sperms' chances of combining successfully with an ovum.

Finding out what happens to sperm inside your partner's body is effected through the postcoital test (see page 45). Although it is your partner who visits the doctor for the test, it is just as much a test of your fertility as it is of hers. In fact it provides a useful assessment of your *combined* fertility by enabling the doctor to examine how well your sperm survive in your partner's body. This is a very important point – in a number of infertile couples both partners are found to be perfectly normal and apparently fertile, but for various reasons the sperm do not survive, or lose their motility and become sluggish, when they come into contact with the cervical mucus. This is often referred to as *combined factor infertility*.

In the postcoital test, as explained before, a small sample of cervical mucus is taken for examination within a few hours of intercourse. Under the microscrope the doctor can see whether sperm are present, how many there are and whether they are active or dead. At this stage the latter is far more important than their numbers. In general, if the results of the postcoital test are good, further investigations will concentrate on your partner. But if the majority of sperm are not moving freely, the reasons must be investigated.

If your seminalysis has been found to be normal, then the cervical mucus is probably to blame. There are several reasons why cervical mucus may be hostile to sperm. First, the mucus may be too acid, or there may be not be enough of it. Sperm are happiest in a slightly alkaline environment. The quantity of mucus secreted by the cervix, and its *pH value* (degree of acidity or alkalinity) vary throughout the menstrual cycle. It is most alkaline and most abundant at the time of ovulation. If the postcoital test is performed at the time of ovulation and the mucus is still found to be unfavourable, its quality and alkalinity can sometimes be improved by giving your partner oestrogen hormones during the first half of her menstrual cycle.

Another reason for a poor postcoital test result is infection of the cervix. In this case the mucus may be cloudy in appearance. Appropriate antibiotics will be prescribed, and the postcoital test repeated after the infection has cleared. However, by far the most significant reason for poor sperm motility in the cervical mucus is the presence of antibodies.

Sperm antibodies

It has been known since the beginning of this century that the body can produce antibodies against human sperm. Antibodies are substances that circulate in the blood and body tissues which help the body to destroy foreign 'invaders'. They form an important part of the immune system – our defence mechanism against infection. Normally the substances (*antigens*) which trigger the production of antibodies are disease-causing organisms such as bacteria or viruses. But occasionally something is not quite right, and some women produce antibodies against their partners' spermatazoa.

We do not yet understand how this happens. In fact it might be more accurate to say that we do not yet understand how it is that in the normal course of events a woman's body does *not* respond to sperm as it would to other foreign cells, that is by producing antibodies! But whatever the mechanism involved, if a woman produces antibodies against the man's sperm, fertility is likely to be impaired. At the postcoital test, adequate numbers of sperm will be seen but they will be dead, having been immobilized by the antibodies.

It is perhaps more surprising to discover that the seminal fluid of some men contains antibodies against their own sperm. In fact, if men did not have special cells to protect their sperm from being exposed to their immune systems, sperm would automatically be destroyed as they are what is called 'antigenically different' – that is, likely to stimulate antibody reaction. If there is some breakdown in this protective system, antibodies may appear in the man's blood and sometimes in the genital secretions. These antibodies can render sperm ineffective by causing them to clump together (*agglutinate*).

Various tests can be performed following the postcoital test to confirm evidence of the presence of antibodies. The most important of these is the sperm-cervical mucus contact test, or

SCMC. This consists of mixing a tiny drop of your semen with a little of your partner's cervical mucus taken just before the time of ovulation, and examining the mixture under a microscope. When antibodies are present, sperm are seen to display a shaking or jerking movement, quite distinct from the normal progressive movement through the mucus. Repeating the test using semen from a donor can identify which partner may be producing antibodies.

Treatments

There are several possible treatments for antisperm antibodies, none of which it has to be said is entirely satisfactory as yet. Antibodies are sometimes produced by men with an infection of the prostate gland; long-term antibiotics can help. A few successes have also been achieved by 'washing' sperm free of antibodies in the laboratory and then introducing them into the woman's uterus by artificial insemination or *in vitro* fertilization (see pages 102 and 109). Treatment with anti-inflammatory hormones (*steroids*) may also reduce the number of antibodies and produce occasional pregnancies.

This is one of the areas of infertility into which the most intensive research is being done, and we must hope that as knowledge of the subject increases, so the outlook for infertile couples with these particular problems will brighten.

Biopsy of the testicles

Some surgeons offer the infertile man in whom no obvious cause of infertility has been found a testicular biopsy and exploration. The object of this is to rule out the possibility of disease or obstruction inside the testes. However, testicular biopsies are often normal and give no clue as to the cause of infertility. In addition, the abnormalities which are found often cannot be corrected. On top of which there is a small but definite risk that sperm production may be suppressed after a testicular biopsy.

Drug treatment

For men with a low sperm count, drug treatment may be advised. However, little real progress has so far been made, although the amount of research conducted throughout the world does give considerable hope for the near future.

Most of the current research centres on the role of hormones. Some doctors prescribe extra male sex hormones (*androgens*) but these are only effective in about half the men treated this way. Another treatment involves the stimulation of the sperm-producing cells by the natural hormone from the pituitary known as follicle-stimulating hormone (FSH). Repeated injections of this hormone have proved to be of some benefit to men with low sperm counts.

Further research is currently being conducted into the use of *clomiphene*, an anti-oestrogen drug, in male infertility following its success in female infertility (see page 88). Similar research is being done into the use of *bromocriptine* (see page 64), which in men lowers levels of prolactin in the blood. High levels of prolactin appear to be associated with low sperm counts, but so far only a small number of men have been treated with this so results are far from conclusive.

Although a number of men have responded to these treatments, the long sperm-production cycle of 70 days means that they have to be continued for periods of six months or more. It is not possible to say how each individual man will respond to the treatment either, but most experts agree that it is of little use for the man with little or no sperm production at all.

Another hormone treatment is with injections of the hormone *testosterone*. This has the effect of suppressing sperm production for a while, in the hopes that when treatment is stopped, the sperm count will rise (*rebound*) to higher concentrations than before the treatment started. One study reported a pregnancy rate of 29 per cent after this treatment, but others are not so optimistic.

The future for male infertility

Major advances in the treatment of male infertility will not be made until many fundamental questions about the subject have been answered more fully. For the man with adequate sperm production, the field of immunology would seem to be throwing up the sort of answers which might assist in this area. For the man with nil or very limited sperm production, the outlook remains bleak.

It is easy to appreciate that the enormous strides made in the treatment of female infertility have encouraged deep interest in the subject among professionals and public alike. No such strides have been made in male infertility recently and the field may well be under-researched at present. In the meantime many men will be walking away from infertility investigations after being told there is little or nothing that can be done for them.

To a man brought up with the common supposition that infertility always occurs because the woman is 'barren' this comes as a great shock. He will know that his sexual prowess is not at fault, he will have been assured that the problem is common among all sorts of men, and that probably nothing he has done in the past has caused his infertility. Although he knows it is not his 'fault', he will need tremendous help from his partner as he accepts this catastrophe in his life. Perhaps this may be the time to consider artificial insemination by donor (see page 110). This is most definitely not a time for blame or recrimination, but a time 'for better, for worse' – for love and support.

SIX

Further tests for women

When you return for your second interview with the doctor, the results of the temperature charts, postcoital test and seminalysis are usually at hand, and if necessary some planning of further investigations can be made accordingly.

Failure of ovulation

Between 20 and 25 per cent of infertile women have problems with ovulation and it is this area that most clinics will investigate first. Evidence that ovulation is not regular, or even completely non-existent, might come from a history of scanty, irregular or absent menstrual periods, or from temperature charts and the other tests already mentioned (see page 44). But to eliminate any doubt as to whether ovulation is occurring a *serum progesterone* measurement must be taken. This is simply an analysis of the level of the hormone progesterone in the bloodstream, and is done by taking blood samples at the appropriate time in your cycle.

After ovulation the progesterone level rises in order to prepare the body for the pregnancy which may follow (see diagram on page 22). Progesterone levels can be measured by a simple blood test, usually performed on the twenty-first day of the cycle. If the ovum is not fertilized, the level of the hormone falls again, the menstrual period begins and the endometrium plus about 50 to 150 ml of blood are shed. So if the serum progesterone is satisfactorily raised it can be assumed that ovulation really has taken place, and if it is not, the doctor can assume that it has not.

Problems with menstruation

If periods are irregular or scanty, more regular ovulation can usually be introduced by giving one of the fertility drugs. This treatment is discussed in full in a separate chapter (see page 86). However, if you are not menstruating at all, matters are a little more complex, and your doctor will probably undertake tests to rule out serious causes.

Most women who have never had regular, satisfactory periods, or who have never menstruated, consult their doctors long before they get to the point of seeking advice for infertility. The majority of women seeking help with infertility will probably have menstruated normally, or almost normally, at some time in their lives; the periods may then have stopped (for instance, after discontinuing the contraceptive pill) or become irregular or scanty.

Screening for ovulation problems

As well as the usual screening tests such as chest x-ray, skull x-ray (to look at the pituitary gland), tests for adrenal, pituitary and thyroid function, and blood tests to exclude diabetes, in recent years a further very important screening test has been introduced. It has been found that a few women produce an excess of a pituitary hormone called *prolactin*. (Prolactin is the hormone normally released after childbirth which stimulates the glands in the breast to produce milk.) In some women this abnormally high prolactin level in the blood causes the breasts to secrete a little fluid and interfere with the periods. Other women have raised prolactin levels without breast discharge and period problems.

The prolactin level can be measured by a blood test. An excess of prolactin is frequently associated with a small tumour of the pituitary gland, so skull x-rays and scans are ordered immediately if a raised prolactin level is found. And now for the good news: the drug called *bromocriptine* can lower raised prolactin levels, so that infertility resulting from such raised levels can be reversed. Many pregnancies have been made possible by this drug in the past fifteen years.

If the supplementary tests described above reveal some more general disorder, for example thyroid disease, this will be treated and your periods observed for the return of normal ovulation, before any further specific infertility treatment is carried out.

But what if you are ovulating normally, but still cannot conceive a child? There are a number of conditions which will then be investigated.

Endometriosis

Endometriosis is a fairly common condition which is often associated with infertility, especially if ovulation is satisfactory. Very simply, specks or blobs of endometrial cells (the cells lining the inside of the uterus) can appear elsewhere in the body – inside the muscle of the uterus, on the ovaries and even on the surface of other pelvic organs such as the bladder and large bowel.

Like the cells inside the uterus, these abnormal blobs of endometrium respond to the hormones produced during the menstrual cycle – they enlarge and may even bleed a little at period times. The periods are also affected – they may be prolonged and irregular, and painful too. Endometriosis tends to occur in women who are in their thirties and forties, but occasionally in younger women too. These women usually have not had a pregnancy. The effects on fertility of even a few endometriotic spots in the pelvis can be marked. As many women, especially working women, are tending to delay starting their families until their late twenties and thirties, endometriosis as a cause of infertility might become more and more common.

If you come within this age group and have had irregular, painful periods, and on examination are found to have tenderness and thickening of the supporting ligaments of the

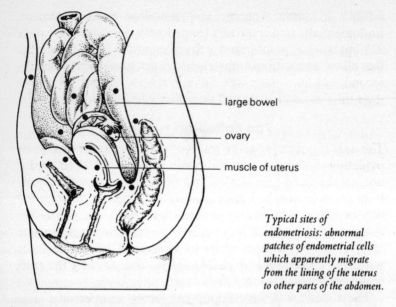

large bowel

ovary

muscle of uterus

*Typical sites of
endometriosis: abnormal
patches of endometrial cells
which apparently migrate
from the lining of the uterus
to other parts of the abdomen.*

uterus, you might well be suspected of having endometriosis. The diagnosis is usually confirmed at laparoscopy (see page 72) when these spots can actually be seen.

There are several possible reasons why these spots appear in the pelvic area, and even so they may only be part of the whole story. Probably the most easily understood and popular explanation is the 'retrograde menstruation' theory – that cells from the lining of the uterus pass upwards into the Fallopian tubes and out into the pelvic cavity instead of down through the cervix and vagina at the menstrual period. These cells produce powerful hormone-like substances called *prostaglandins*, and these may interfere with the ovum after ovulation.

There are many questions about endometriosis still to be answered but an important fact is now at hand. Elaborate studies have shown that even a small area of endometriosis, just a few black speckles (which are described as resembling a powder burn from a gun), can exert a profound effect on fertility in some women, and therefore need treatment. Endometriosis is successfully treated with hormones (see page 92), but two last points are worthy of mention. First, remember that all women with endometriosis are not necessarily infertile; second, not all women who have irregular, painful periods in their thirties and forties will necessarily have endometriosis.

The Fallopian tubes

The next big question to be resolved after you are shown to be ovulating is whether your Fallopian tubes are blocked, and if not, are the lining cells working properly, or are they damaged? If an ovum is fertilized after ovulation, it stays in the tube for two or three days before passing down into the uterus for implantation. The Fallopian tube is more than just a pipeline carrying the ovum from ovary to uterus; the delicate ovum is nurtured, protected and guided for several days by the cells lining the tubes.

The tubes are a very important factor in infertility. The lining, and the whole tube itself, can be damaged by infection, especially if it goes untreated or is treated inadequately. Scarring can result from these infections, although not, of course, in every case. High on the list of infections which can cause tube damage is the venereal disease gonorrhoea. Infection following abdominal surgery such as having your appendix removed may also affect the tube, and perhaps bind it down in adhesions. An ectopic pregnancy in the tube may have been removed in the past, along with a portion of tube. And a history of pelvic infection will also focus your doctor's attention on the state of the Fallopian tubes.

Checking for tubal patency
The first line of investigation will be to see, by means of a laparoscopy, if the tubes are open (*patent*) or blocked (see page 75). This is where couples will have to steel themselves to face the prospect of a series of clinic visits and occasional stays in

The hysterosalpingogram

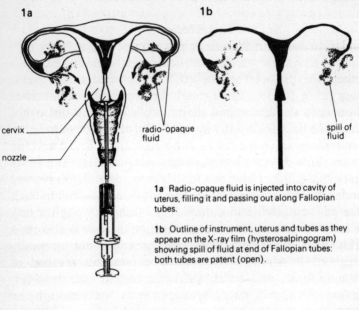

cervix

nozzle

radio-opaque fluid

spill of fluid

1a Radio-opaque fluid is injected into cavity of uterus, filling it and passing out along Fallopian tubes.

1b Outline of instrument, uterus and tubes as they appear on the X-ray film (hysterosalpingogram) showing spill of fluid at end of Fallopian tubes: both tubes are patent (open).

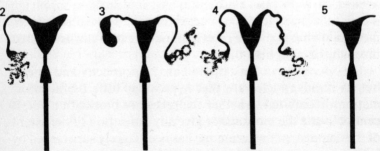

2 Right-hand Fallopian tube is open but left tube blocked at entrance to uterus.

3 Right-hand tube is sac-like and blocked (hydrosalpinx).

4 Both tubes are open but uterus has a divided cavity (septate or bicornuate uterus).

5 Right tube is blocked close to uterus, left tube blocked half way along its length.

hospital on the part of the woman. Many couples find this tedious, but it is important to keep in mind that everyone is working towards the ultimate goal of a successful pregnancy.

Insufflation

Insufflation is the rather descriptive name for a fairly old-fashioned technique which is still occasionally used to establish whether tubes are open or blocked. In this procedure, the idea is to pass gas under pressure through the uterus, Fallopian tubes and out into the abdominal cavity, while listening through a stethoscope held against the woman's low abdomen to hear the gas bubbling out of the tubes. If no gas can be heard and the pressure remains quite high then it is assumed that both tubes are blocked. If gas cannot be heard on one side and the pressure is moderately high, then the tubes on one side could be blocked.

The gas, usually carbon dioxide, is passed through a tiny tube inserted through the vagina. Carbon dioxide is absorbed quickly into the bloodstream and breathed out normally through the lungs. If your doctor chooses this method of investigation you may be left with some pain in your shoulder, as the gas may have irritated the diaphragm. Oddly enough, the sensory nerves of the shoulder are the same as those supplying the diaphragm so the pain is 'referred' to the shoulder area. In fact this pain is a good sign as it shows that the gas has passed through the Fallopian tubes.

The advantages of insufflation are its simplicity and safety, but its disadvantages are that it provides little useful information. It only tells whether the tubes are blocked or not; it cannot locate the blockage or give any indication of the extent of the damage, so the technique has been largely superseded by laparoscopy.

Hysterosalpingogram

If your doctor suspects that there might be some developmental or other abnormality of the uterus and/or Fallopian tubes, he or she might suggest an x-ray investigation called a *hysterosalpingogram*. Most doctors refer to this less cumbersomely as an HSG. The abnormalities being looked for may be an abnormally shaped uterus (which may cause repeated miscarriage), or one that is severely distorted by fibroids.

An HSG is usually performed while you are awake, although a few doctors prefer to use a general anaesthetic. The procedure is not without some discomfort, but usually does not produce severe pain. It involves gently injecting a liquid into the uterus through the cervical canal. The liquid fills the uterus, outlining its inner shape, and can be seen on the x-ray, while the pelvis is observed under an x-ray image intensifier. This filling of the uterus can cause cramping, like an intense menstrual pain.

The liquid is watched as it enters the Fallopian tubes and spills into the abdominal cavity. The site of any blockage is noted as well as the shape of the uterus. The actual x-ray filming takes two or three minutes but the whole procedure is likely to take about 10 minutes and is often combined with an *endometrial biopsy*, when a tiny piece of the lining of the uterus is removed for laboratory examination. Every precaution is of course taken beforehand to make sure you are not already pregnant at the time of the HSG.

Any abnormality of the uterus can be detected, and if possible the doctor may arrange to have it surgically corrected at a later date. However, abnormal shape does not always affect fertility. More important is the manifestation of any blockage in the Fallopian tubes. However, the HSG gives little information about the state of the tubes themselves, and if the blockage is very close to the uterus it does not show the rest of the tube at all, and any 'kinking' of the tube shows up only rarely. It is because of its limitations that HSG has largely been replaced by laparoscopy but it is still used for locating tubal blockages and uterine abnormality.

As with many procedures in infertility work, HSG is sometimes followed by an unexpected pregnancy. Many doctors in this field can quote dozens of examples where a woman has conceived soon after having an HSG. This may be due to the relief of anxiety that a normal HSG brings, or it may be that the oily liquid used may flush out the tubes in some way, perhaps dividing the tiny adhesions inside the tubes that in some cases are responsible for infertility. While this is a very welcome side effect for the lucky few women who enjoy a pregnancy assisted in some way by an HSG, it must be emphasised that the HSG is primarily an investigation and not a treatment!

SEVEN

Laparoscopy

Modern technology has ensured that doctors can now look directly at a woman's uterus and Fallopian tubes and inspect them for problems concerning infertility, through the use of an instrument called a *laparoscope*. The word means roughly a 'telescope in the abdomen', from the Greek *lapar*, loin or flank. The technique is so important and its use so widespread that it deserves a chapter to itself.

How laparoscopy is carried out

Laparoscopy is always performed in hospital; it can be carried out under local anaesthetic but the procedure is usually quicker and offers little discomfort if you are given a general anaesthetic so that you are fully unconscious. During the operation a thin hollow needle (known as a *Verres needle*) is inserted into your abdomen, which is inflated with a controlled supply of carbon dioxide or nitrous oxide gas, raising the abdominal muscles away from the intestines and pelvic organs. This provides a space in which the laparoscope can be manoeuvred with safety and ease.

When sufficient gas has been passed and the abdominal wall is dome-shaped, the laparoscope is inserted. The instrument itself is a sort of telescope, about 5 to 10 mm in diameter, which has a passage to keep a small flow of gas passing into the abdomen, replacing any losses, as well as a fibre-optic light source.

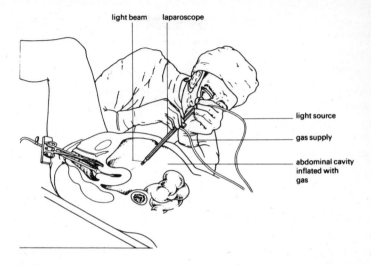

light beam   laparoscope

light source

gas supply

abdominal cavity
inflated with
gas

During laparoscopy the surgeon can observe the Fallopian tubes as dye is squirted through the uterus and escapes through the Fallopian tubes.

What the doctor looks for

The initial appearance of your pelvic area may suggest previous pelvic infections (or even current infections), particularly if there are adhesions – bands of scar tissue. A common site for these is the right side of the pelvis where they may occur as a result of appendicitis. The bowel is also observed, especially for signs of infection such as Crohn's disease (a chronic inflammatory condition of the bowel).

Your doctor will be looking for a satisfactory round or pear-shaped uterus and will also be anxious to rule out any congenital abnormalities of the uterus. The uterine shape may commonly be distorted by fibroids – non-malignant tumours of the uterine muscle. All the above conditions may be causes of infertility.

The doctor will then turn to the state of the ovaries, to see whether they are both present and have an appearance suggesting normal function. Absence of one ovary is rare and

Problems diagnosed by laparoscopy

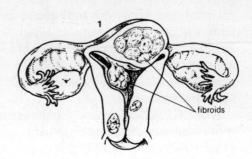

1 Fibroids (non-malignant tumours) can form in the uterine cavity, in the myometrium (muscle), or beneath the surface.

fibroids

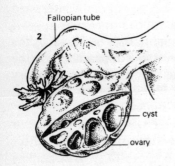

Fallopian tube

cyst

ovary

2 Polycystic ovaries. Multiple cysts form in the periphery of the ovary with excess stroma in between.

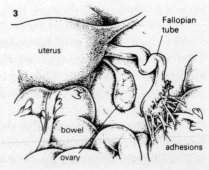

Fallopian tube

uterus

bowel

ovary

adhesions

3 Adhesions, in this case binding down the fimbrial ends of the right Fallopian tube and stuck to the large bowel (caecum).

does not usually cause infertility if the other is working normally. However, the doctor may see evidence of the *polycystic ovary syndrome*. In this condition, the ovaries are enlarged and filled with multiple cysts. This syndrome interferes with ovulation but can often be cured by surgery or fertility drug treatment (see page 86). Polycystic ovaries can appear relatively normal at laparoscopy – the diagnosis may then be made later by ultrasound scanning, along with hormone blood tests.

A careful search is made for the presence of brown or black spots suggesting endometriosis. This condition is a prime cause of infertility (see page 65), but can be successfully treated in the majority of cases.

During laparoscopy your doctor will be especially interested in the Fallopian tubes. Their overall appearance may suggest previous infection (*salpingitis*). Salpingitis may be shown by the presence of adhesions and an abnormal appearance of the covering layer of the tube. Adhesions may bind down the ovary preventing release of an ovum, or block the tube itself, and infection can also destroy the tube lining.

Adhesions of the pelvis or abdomen form to a greater or lesser extent after any surgery, but pelvic adhesions may affect the reproductive organs and thus impair fertility. If adhesions bind down the tubes, it is difficult for an ovum to pass down them, so the doctor will spend some time examining the tubes closely to make sure they are fully mobile.

Testing for tubal patency

The next step is to see whether the tubes are *patent*, or open along their entire length. This can be shown by filling the uterus with dark-coloured water-soluble dye. If the tubes are open, the dye will pass along them and spill into the abdominal cavity at the ends. The passage of the dye along the inside of the tube can be seen through the laparoscope, since the outside of the tube will be slightly darkened by the dye. If the tube is blocked, the site of the obstruction can often be located. If the tube is completely blocked, or blocked near the junction with the uterus, no dye will pass at all.

Endometrial biopsy

After the dye has been passed and tubal function assessed, a curettage of the uterus may be performed. This allows the doctor to take a sample of the lining of the uterus – an *endometrial biopsy* – with a spoon-like instrument called a *curette*. Some doctors take an endometrial biopsy at the time of the physical examination (see page 41) to check whether ovulation has occurred. But if there is still any doubt at the time of the laparoscopy then an endometrial biopsy at this stage will settle the issue.

Completing laparoscopy

The whole procedure of laparoscopy, passing dye and endometrial biopsy is normally completed within half an hour, and yields a great deal of information about the state of the reproductive organs. A surgeon is able to assess whether operations such as surgery to repair the Fallopian tubes, removal of fibroids or removal of adhesions are feasible so that he or she can discuss the pros and cons with you before embarking on further surgery.

Sometimes the doctor will suggest beforehand that if he or she discovers the need for tubal surgery during laparoscopy the work could be done immediately following the inspection. However, tubal surgery can take as much as two hours and the operating theatre would normally have to be booked in advance, so in most cases you will be booked in for tubal surgery at a later date.

Laparoscopy by itself is relatively safe, and most people are able to leave hospital quite soon after the operation. Many women return home after as little as three to six hours' observation, although most stay in hospital overnight. Complaints afterwards are few but may include those resulting from the anaesthetic (sore throat, general muscle aches, nausea) and those caused by the laparoscope itself (painful navel, menstrual cramps, vaginal bleeding). If any gas remains in the abdomen it is usually absorbed slowly into the bloodstream. Occasionally, however, it will rise to the top of the abdomen and irritate the diaphragm. Since the sensory nerves to the diaphragm also supply the skin over the tip to the shoulder, pain from such diaphragmatic irritation is felt in the shoulder – usually passing within a day or so.

EIGHT

Miscarriage

I have included miscarriage in this book, which is essentially about overcoming infertility, with reservation. Infertility is really about inability to conceive, whereas miscarriage can occur only after you have become pregnant. However, the aim of all infertility treatment is not simple pregnancy, but a live baby. Miscarriage may show that you can conceive, but the end result is the same as infertility – an empty cot. In fact nowadays many women who have had troubles with miscarriage are investigated and treated in infertility clinics.

Terminology

There are a lot of different terms relating to miscarriage. Doctors tend to use them, sometimes offhandedly, as if everyone knows their exact meaning, and this can cause confusion and even distress. For a start, doctors do not usually use the term miscarriage at all – they say 'abortion'. However, since this word is used by most people to mean a deliberately induced termination of pregnancy rather than the accidental loss of a fetus, I shall use the term miscarriage to avoid confusion. At present in the United Kingdom a fetus is not considered viable (that is, capable of life outside his or her mother's womb) if born before 28 weeks of pregnancy (about 6 months). However since many special care baby units are able to save some babies born at less than 28 weeks this arbitrary age limit is under review.

Most miscarriages, whether early or late, follow or are

accompanied by bleeding through the vagina. Bleeding in pregnancy before 28 weeks heralds a possible miscarriage and is referred to medically as a *threatened abortion*. If this happens, the mother is usually advised to rest in bed (not necessarily in hospital – that depends on how far along the pregnancy has progressed) and is monitored by the obstetrician to look for possible causes of the bleeding. However if the cervix opens and the mother experiences pain from uterine contractions (mini-labour pains) the fetus will eventually be passed out. At this stage doctors speak of an *inevitable abortion*. Once the fetus and placenta have been passed, the term is a *complete abortion* but if some bits and pieces remain in the uterus it is called an *incomplete abortion*.

Induced (therapeutic) abortion

As I have already said the majority of miscarriages are spontaneous. They can occur out of the blue – not after falling over, not after emotional upsets, not after any specific event – they just happen. Although there are circumstances when miscarriage may be triggered by a severe blow to the abdomen, or a very high fever, the vast majority of miscarriages have no exterior cause.

However miscarriage procured by interference inside the uterus or by taking poisonous drugs has been a feature of human society throughout history. Induced abortion, as it is called, performed within the confines of the law, in approved medical institutions, is often referred to as *therapeutic abortion* or as TOP – *termination of pregnancy*.

Induced abortion, even when performed in the first few weeks of pregnancy in experienced medical centres, can be followed by infection which may also result in infertility if not properly treated.

The danger of infection

An incomplete abortion is a dangerous situation if not treated promptly. If either the dead fetus or the placenta, or even part of the membrane, remain inside the uterus after miscarriage there is a serious risk of infection. This would be called a *septic abortion*, and in the days before antibiotics this condition was frequently fatal. That is why after a miscarriage, the doctor will recommend that your uterus is gently scraped out under general anaesthetic within several hours of the miscarriage. If your temperature remains normal and there is no excessive vaginal bleeding afterwards, you would be allowed home within a day.

Infection following a miscarriage can affect fertility afterwards. As you can imagine, virulent infection inside the womb is bound to affect the Fallopian tubes to a greater or lesser extent, and tubal blockage or damage may result, as it may from other types of infection discussed in earlier chapters. However, in the vast majority of cases miscarriage does *not* impair fertility, and many thousands of women may experience one or more miscarriages – always a traumatic and disappointing occurrence – yet bear several healthy babies as well.

Causes of early miscarriage

About one pregnancy in five or six ends in miscarriage in the United Kingdom. When you consider how many pregnancies there are every year, even in those Western countries with zero population growth, you can appreciate that an enormous number of miscarriages must take place. A large proportion of those – up to 60 per cent – occur because there is something wrong with the baby, frequently a chromosomal abnormality. The body detects that the pregnancy is defective and the quicker that it passes out of the mother's body the better.

In some miscarriages the fetus fails to develop at all and an empty sac is passed out of the uterus. This is referred to as a *blighted ovum* or *missed abortion* – terms of which I and many others are not particularly fond, as they imply that there is some disease at work. In many cases, in fact, it is again a question of a mistake in the chromosomal construction. Miscarriage in this event can be thought of as a quality control procedure.

Another factor in miscarriage is the failure of the embryo, although perfectly all right in itself, to implant properly in the lining of the uterus. Alternatively it may implant in a position which makes miscarriage likely – low down in the uterus. This may be a result of hormonal failure. Hormones may be at insufficient levels to prepare the lining or sustain the embryo properly.

The pregnancy is initially supported by the hormones produced from the corpus luteum in the ovary (see page 20) but early in pregnancy production of these hormones is handed over to the placenta. If this hand-over of hormone production is ill-timed or inadequate, a drop in hormone levels results, and is followed by miscarriage. This theory is not completely proven but it explains why progesterone-type hormones are occasionally given to women with threatened miscarriage, for whatever reason.

Occasionally miscarriage may be due to conditions suffered by the mother such as kidney problems or very high blood pressure. However, infection is much more likely through conditions such as rubella (German measles), poliomyelitis and other viral infections, or bacterial infections such as tuberculosis, syphilis, toxoplasmosis and listeriosis and, in places where the disease is endemic, malaria. Let me stress that these are uncommon causes, but where they are suspected, the doctor will treat the mother accordingly.

It has also been suggested that what you eat might be implicated in certain miscarriages. Although the evidence is not conclusive, it may be that certain vitamin deficiencies could be a cause, in particular a lack of folic acid.

A possible explanation for a very small number of miscarriages is that the mother rejects her own fetus. One example of this is the rhesus factor – when a sensitized rhesus-negative mother 'attacks' a rhesus-positive fetus in her uterus. The process is a very complicated one, involving the mother's immune system. Just as men have a special mechanism which enables their bodies not to reject their sperm (see page 59) so women have a mechanism which overrides their immune system to stop it from rejecting the fetus. If this breaks down the fetus would be rejected and a miscarriage would result.

Treating early miscarriage

Although you may not want to try for another baby straight away, your doctor may advise you to wait three or four months and then try again. He is unlikely to consider treating you until you had had three or more miscarriages in a row. This is known as recurrent or habitual miscarriage.

It is not unnatural to want to know why this is happening to you, especially as it is both emotionally and physically draining. But in many cases, your doctor will be unable to say. Examination of the miscarried fetus under the microscope may indicate chromosomal or other congenital problems, but in all too many women no definite cause is found. However, an attempt will be made to rule out as many causes as possible, with blood tests for infections, antibodies, thyroid function, diabetes and other conditions, and you will be treated appropriately.

If hormone deficiencies are suspected, there is in most cases little that can be done, as giving women hormones has not proved to help a great deal. Hormone deficiency implies that the placenta is failing, but the drop in hormones may well be a side-effect rather than a prime cause of the problem.

Threatened miscarriage is usually dealt with by bed rest, often in hospital, in the hope that the bleeding will settle down. During these anxious days of waiting it is not surprising that some women plead for something more active in the way of treatment to save their pregnancies. Occasionally, doctors will prescribe hormones such as progestogens. These will be given as much to reassure them as anything.

If you are showing signs of a threatened miscarriage, you will probably be given ultrasound scans to check whether the fetus is still alive. If movement is detected, then every effort will be made to conserve the pregnancy, but if not, then two or three days of unnecessary and anxious waiting in hospital can be avoided, and an immediate operation performed to remove the contents of the womb safely and under general anaesthetic.

Causes of late miscarriage

Miscarriage later in the pregnancy is usually a problem of accommodation. An abnormally shaped uterus may account for late miscarriage. The embryo implants well but the growing baby cannot be held inside the abnormal uterus. An abnormal uterus is sometimes found to be the cause of repeated miscarriages, and if this happens to you you will probably be offered corrective surgery following an HSG (see pages 70 and 97).

Another cause of late miscarriage is *incompetent cervix*. After the first three months of pregnancy the weight of the fetus presses down on the cervix, so if it is *incompetent* (weak) and starts to open up, there is a danger that miscarriage will occur through simple mechanical failure. What usually happens is that the bag of waters (*amniotic fluid*) bulges through the gap in the open cervix and the membranes rupture, with miscarriage inevitably following. This would probably happen (usually without warning) at around the sixteenth to twentieth week of pregnancy, although the cervix may hold until later in the pregnancy when your baby would be born prematurely.

Cervical incompetence has various causes. The sort of factors which can lead to a degree of cervical incompetence in some cases (but by no means all) are weakening through previous deliveries of babies, sometimes through late terminations of pregnancy, sometimes through operations to the cervix, such as cone biopsy.

Left: HSG of a normal cervix. Right: HSG of an incompetent cervix, showing the classic funnel shape.

Treating late miscarriage

The causes of late miscarriage are usually mechanical and therefore treatable. Uterine abnormalities are dealt with surgically (see page 97); incompetent cervix is also treated surgically with a purse-string suture (frequently a strong, narrow tape) inserted around the neck of the womb. It is inserted under a general anaesthetic when you are about 14 weeks pregnant, and therefore past the time when an early miscarriage is likely, but before the time that the baby and placenta are heavy enough to push the cervix open. The suture is removed at about 38 weeks of pregnancy and labour usually follows soon afterwards.

If you show signs of a late threatened miscarriage, usually by vaginal bleeding, you will almost certainly be admitted to the antenatal ward of the nearest hospital with an up-to-date special care baby unit. For a start the bleeding may be due to other causes, such as *placenta praevia* (the term given to the placenta when it is attached to the lower part of the uterus), and in any case bed-rest at this stage may enable the pregnancy to be sustained at least until the time the baby could be cared for in an incubator. In this situation you might be given drugs to inhibit uterine contractions as well.

Psychological support

If you experience a threatened or actual miscarriage you will need a lot of support from your partner, family and friends, and from the medical team helping you. Above all, misplaced feelings of guilt need to be overcome, and a couple, especially the woman, must be allowed to grieve for the lost baby just as they would the death of any child born to them. However, it has to be said that it is very difficult to find ways to reassure someone who has had five or six miscarriages for which no cause can be found.

NINE

Switching on ovulation

Problems with ovulation account for the failure to conceive in about 10 to 15 per cent of infertile couples. Fortunately the treatment of women who fail to ovulate is very successful and the prospects for you if you are *anovulatory*, to use the medical term, are good. In recent years several drugs to induce ovulation have become available – the so-called 'fertility drugs', which act by stimulating the ovaries to produce eggs.

Contrary to the impression you might get from stories in the tabloids, the risks of multiple births from fertility drugs are quite low. In fact there are two stages of drug treatment and the second stage, which carries a higher risk of multiple births, is only begun if you fail to respond to the first stage, and careful monitoring by the medical team minimizes the danger.

There are various ways of testing whether you are ovulating or not, and one of the most obvious of these is lack of menstruation (*amenorrhoea*). Basically, the requirements for normal ovulation and menstruation are a normal uterus and ovaries, and the release of hormones from the pituitary gland to stimulate the ovaries. There can be any number of reasons why your periods may stop (leaving aside pregnancy, of course). It could be that your uterus is misshapen or damaged by infection; an ovary could be unresponsive because of polycystic disease or premature menopause; but most frequently the fault lies with the pituitary gland or its 'boss', the hypothalamus, which is situated directly above it in the brain, and which between them control the hormones associated with reproduction.

Unusual causes of amenorrhoea

Pituitary gland/hypothalamus causes of amenorrhoea have already been outlined on pages 33 and 64, and their treatment is with drugs. But before discussing hormone treatment, there are some rarer causes which need to be ruled out. First, premature menopause is an unfortunate cause for some women under 40. The menopause, which is the time when a woman's reproductive time comes to an end, normally occurs at around the age of 50, although there is considerable variation either side. However, if the menopause is suddenly triggered during a woman's thirties, or even younger, it is deemed premature.

It is usually discovered with the aid of an ovarian biopsy and the finding of raised levels of FSH (follicle-stimulating hormone) in the blood, but regrettably little or nothing can be done for women who wish to conceive after premature menopause. The causes are not entirely known, but may be associated with the failure of other endocrine glands (adrenal, thyroid, pancreas), possibly due to an immunity to one's own tissue (*auto-immunity*).

Polycystic ovaries may also account for amenorrhoea. Diagnosis is made by ultrasound scanning which reveals the many little cysts inside the ovary and by measuring levels of FSH and LH (see page 88) in the blood. It may be treated removing a wedge of tissue from each ovary in an operation known as *wedge resection*.

If your periods do not start again after discontinuing the contraceptive pill (post-pill amenorrhoea) or if your amenorrhoea is of an unknown cause, you will normally be treated with fertility drugs to stimulate ovulation, as described below.

The progesterone challenge

If you are found not to be ovulating but everything else is normal, your doctor usually starts treatment by creating an artificial period from which future fertility drug treatment can be dated. Sex hormones, usually synthetic progestogen similar to natural progesterone, are given in the form of tablets for about five days. Alternatively a single injection of progesterone may be given. Either way a withdrawal menstrual bleed usually follows within a week as the body is tricked into acting as if ovulation had taken place.

The first day of bleeding can then be counted as Day 1 of the artificial cycle and further treatment measured from there. As well as producing a starting base the period produced by this so-called 'progesterone challenge' gives an indication that the uterus and endometrium are responding reasonably well to the presence of the hormone. In someone whose uterus has been severely damaged by infection, for example, the response to the challenge will be negative – no period will ensue, and further investigations will be required.

Inducing ovulation

At this point, you will be having a menstrual period but not ovulating. What is required is a drug which will 'switch on' the pituitary gland and cause it to produce the natural hormones necessary to stimulate the ovaries into producing a ripe ovum. (The same treatment would be given if you did have periods, but were still found not to be ovulating.)

The drug frequently chosen for this is *clomiphene citrate*, although more recently *tamoxifen* has also come into use. Clomiphene reduces the uptake of oestrogen by the pituitary gland and hypothalamus, and the pituitary subsequently releases what are known as *gonadotrophin* hormones (luteinizing hormone and follicle-stimulating hormone – LH and FSH) to stimulate the ovaries. The fertility drugs are thus acting on the body's hormonal feedback system, by which the pituitary and hypothalamus monitor the levels of hormones in the blood and release more hormones as necessary.

Their action is in fact the very reverse of the action of the oral contraceptive pill, which introduces *extra* oestrogen into the body, tricking the body into thinking it is pregnant so inhibiting ovulation. The fertility drugs are 'anti-oestrogens', which in effect are shouting to the lazy pituitary gland that not enough hormones are being secreted and not enough ova have been released by the ovaries. There is some evidence that clomiphene also has a direct effect on the ovaries, but the simplest way to regard clomiphene and tamoxifen is as agents which stimulate the pituitary gland to start the cycle.

Administering clomiphene

There may be some variation in the dose, duration and timing of clomiphene administration from doctor to doctor, but the underlying principle remains the same. To give an example, one tablet (50 mg) per day is given on Days 2 to 6, or Days 5 to 10, of the cycle. If after one month you have not menstruated, or a pregnancy has not been produced (this is a very real possibility – I know of several women who have conceived after just one course of tablets), the dose can be doubled and trebled subsequently if necessary.

The doctor will watch for evidence of ovulation using temperature charts and Day 21 serum progesterone tests (see page 63). If ovulation does occur around the middle of the cycle (Day 14 or so), clomiphene is continued cyclically at the right dose level for your circumstances, and you will be encouraged to have intercourse at the appropriate time in your cycle.

In these relatively small doses and short courses of treatment, over-stimulation of the ovaries is unusual, but some doctors will want to check by vaginal examination that the ovaries are not enlarged before each course of clomiphene. If enlargement is detected, it may mean that too many follicles have been stimulated at the same time so drug treatment will be suspended until the swelling settles down, which usually takes about a month.

Side effects from clomiphene are not common, but a small percentage of women have reported occasional hot flushes, similar to those experienced during the menopause, while they are taking the drug and for a few days after. However, the same person may not experience these symptoms during every treatment cycle and hardly any women are completely unable to take this effective treatment.

Effective treatment it is indeed – it produces viable ovulation in about three-quarters of women with secondary amenorrhoea (especially 'post-pill' amenorrhoea) and with the polycystic ovary syndrome. About a quarter of women with primary amenorrhoea (in other words, who have never menstruated) will also ovulate. Pregnancy, however, is the ultimate yardstick by which to judge the effectiveness of treatment. Provided you are healthy and failure of ovulation is the only problem affecting your fertility, most doctors would expect a 50 per cent chance of conception.

Direct stimulation of the ovaries

If your doctor finds that treatment with clomiphene or tamoxifen is unsuccessful, you may well be considered for treatment with gonadotrophins. This consists of injections with FSH which will directly induce the ovary to produce a ripe ovum. The treatment is complex, expensive, needs careful monitoring and carries an ever-present risk of over-stimulation of the ovaries, producing discomfort and a high chance of multiple births. Consequently this treatment is not something to be embarked upon lightly and should only be carried out by experienced doctors in reputable centres, with access to rapid laboratory hormone measurements.

Before you start treatment with gonadotrophins, you and your partner will have been fully investigated to make sure all other possible causes of infertility have been ruled out or treatments ineffective. No doctor would embark on this without a full discussion of the implications with you both as your immediate co-operation is essential. I will only give a brief outline of the treatment as the actual administration of the hormone can vary from one doctor or clinic to another.

The gonadotrophins used have to be natural substances, not synthetic; they are extracted from the pituitary glands of dead bodies (HPG) or, more acceptably and in larger quantities, from the urine of post-menopausal women (HMG). However, it is now possible to obtain pure FSH and this may eventually replace HMG.

In addition, a luteinizing hormone (LH) is required and the one most frequently chosen is *human chorionic gonadotrophin* (HCG) which is secreted in large amounts during pregnancy, and again is present in the urine of pregnant women. Treatment with *human pituitary gonadotrophin* (HMG) or *human menopausal gonadotrophin* (HPG) is usually given in conjunction with HCG.

Basically, a series of injections is given to induce ovulation, but careful measurement of hormone levels in the urine or blood are made to make sure the ovaries are not over-stimulated. Further evidence of response to treatment may also be given by observing your cervical mucus and vaginal tissue to look for the effects of oestrogen. The doctor will increase the dose of HMG or HPG given until satisfied that ovulation has been induced (the dose varies from woman to woman), but if over-stimulation is indicated, then the usual injection of HCG is not given.

The treatment schedule

Let me give you an example of a popular treatment schedule. (The treatment is usually undertaken as an outpatient, so if you live a considerable distance from your clinic, you may need to stay in accommodation nearby.) Three injections of equal doses of HMG are given on three alternate days (Days 1, 3 and 5). On Day 2, a 24-hour urine collection or a blood sample is taken and the level of oestrogen is measured to record a baseline. This is repeated on Day 4 and Day 6, to check that over-stimulation has not occurred, which would be indicated by high oestrogen levels. On Day 8 oestrogen is measured again to provide an indication of the dosage of HMG needed for further courses, if necessary. Also on Day 8, if all is well and your oestrogen level indicates that a ripe ovum is ready to be released, then an injection of HCG is given to induce ovulation. You will then be advised to have intercourse on that day and the following day, in the hope that conception will occur. The ripening of the follicle and the release of the ovum can be monitored by having daily ultrasound scans to watch the follicle swell and then 'pop' when the egg is released.

If all this strikes you as rather complicated, then I have succeeded in giving you an accurate picture: it *is* complicated. It requires a good deal of co-operation between you and your doctor, who really needs to know what he or she is doing. However, the high success rate makes the treatment eminently worthwhile, and with modern ultrasound scanning which can detect not only the release of an ovum, but also if an ovary is being over-stimulated in time to hold back on treatment, the risks of higher multiples than twins are greatly reduced.

Ovulation helped by LH/RH

Some women, especially those with polycystic ovarian syndrome, need treatment with luteinizing hormone releasing substances. These have the effect of 'dampening down' excess ovulation with a clean hormonal sheet, so to speak. LH/RH substances used to be given by a pump but nowadays are taken by nasal spray or injections under the skin.

Ovulation and endometriosis

As has already been seen, endometriosis can interfere quite significantly with female fertility (see page 65). Sometimes the black spots or blobs can be cut out or cauterized in conjunction with laparoscopy, but the most usual treatment is again with hormones. Because the spots of endometrial material are both stimulated by the hormones that trigger menstruation, and themselves produce powerful prostaglandins, the treatment is geared to damping down the hormonal activity which keeps the spots going.

This could be by taking the combined oestrogen-progestogen contraceptive pill every day without a break for six to twelve months. This suppresses periods completely and hopefully eradicates all the spots. It doesn't always work but it is worth trying because it has been shown that there is a higher chance of conceiving if endometriosis is cleared up. There are likely to be a few side-effects, of course, which may include weight gain, water retention, headache, fatigue and breast discomfort. Talk to your doctor if you are worried about these.

An alternative treatment is to suppress the menstrual cycle with a drug called *danazol*, which effects the pituitary gland. Suppression of the periods means that the endometrium, and therefore the endometriotic spots, do not develop and the latter begin to shrink. Danazol has a few side effects too, but these can be minimized by restricting the dose given.

Sometimes you may be offered surgery, even if you are being treated with hormones. Scarring round the Fallopian tubes and ovaries can develop as a reaction to endometriosis so these may need to be removed surgically and any remaining areas of endometriosis cauterized. In any case, if you have not conceived a baby after a year of hormone treatment, you may be given a laparoscopy to see if the endometriosis has completely cleared.

TEN

Corrective surgery

If you are ovulating satisfactorily, and your partner shows evidence of potential fertility, the remaining obstacles to fertility are principally mechanical. The more complicated investigative procedures described earlier may have shown up some of these problems.

The Fallopian tubes

The Fallopian tubes are the most likely site of mechanical failure. Infection, whether directly in the tubes, or indirectly as a result of abdominal operations or pelvic inflammatory disease (PID), can cause blockage or distortion due to adhesions.

If you have been found to be ovulating normally, and your Fallopian tubes shown to be blocked, misshapen or immobilized by adhesions, then it is technically possible to open them up. Note the use of the word 'technically'. Even though the tubes may be opened up or made mobile again, they still may not function properly. It cannot be said too often that they are not just little funnels down which the ovum slides into the uterus. They are designed to provide the site for fertilization and to nurture a fertilized ovum for several days during its passage to the uterus.

The risks of tubal surgery

It is important not to expect too much from tubal surgery as the results can be disappointing even with the most expert of surgical teams using the most up-to-date micro-surgical equipment. Surgery involves a major abdominal operation, involving at least two hours under general anaesthetic, so should not be entered into lightly. Although tubal surgery may open up the tubes, it could in itself cause residual damage, causing a narrowing or blockage in a tube which may subsequently result in an ectopic pregnancy. This in turn means further surgery to remove the embryo, and renders your chances of conceiving subsequently even less.

However, after discussing the pros and cons fully with both of you and with the results of laparoscopy to hand, your doctor may well feel it is worth offering you an operation to restore tubal patency and mobility, but will be quick to point out the risks and the chances of success.

What can be done

Cutting away adhesions is a fairly straightforward procedure, and full mobility of the ovary and tubes can be restored with a 40 per cent chance of subsequent pregnancy. It is sometimes possible also to open out the fimbriae if the blockage is at that end, and if they are destroyed completely there is a technique for making an artificially wide opening of the tube which is occasionally successful. However, if the ends of the tubes are blocked and become swollen with fluid it is severely damaging, and opening them out rarely results in subsequent pregnancy.

If one or both of the tubes does not appear badly damaged, but it is known that the mid-portion is blocked, the diseased segment can be cut out and the two ends joined. However, even though the shortened tube may be patent this operation meets with only limited success, measured by pregnancies produced.

Tubal surgery does, however, meet with some success when the tubes are blocked near to the point where they join the uterus, provided the rest of the tube looks healthy. In this operation the diseased part is cut out and the healthy part re-implanted into the uterus. The muscle of the uterus is cut during

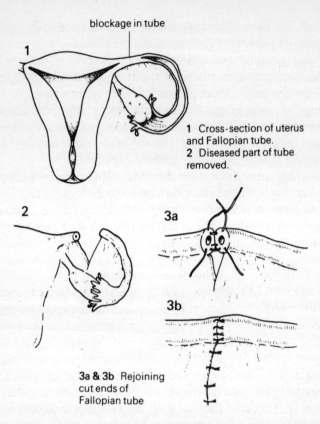

1 Cross-section of uterus and Fallopian tube.
2 Diseased part of tube removed.

3a & 3b Rejoining cut ends of Fallopian tube

A blocked Fallopian tube can be repaired by cutting away the blocked portion and rejoining the patent ends.

this procedure, so you should be prepared for a possible Caesarean section for the birth of any subsequent baby.

To keep the tube open, some surgeons leave little nylon threads inside the tube as 'splints' to be removed when the tube is healed. Others believe that splints may damage the tube lining. Some doctors give steroids during and after the operation to decrease the amount of inflammation after the operation, although their value in these circumstances is not known for sure. The uterus and tubes may also be 'washed through' in the days following the operation.

The medical team will take meticulous care to avoid too much bleeding at the operation and to keep the risk of infection to a minimum. If there is more than a drop or two of blood around, especially inside the Fallopian tube, then adhesions may form, ruining the whole attempt to restore function.

Abnormalities of the uterus

A misshapen uterus may be thought to be a cause of infertility in a very few women. The problem with uterine abnormalities usually lies not so much in becoming pregnant as in holding the pregnancy in (see page 84). Many women with an abnormally shaped womb, of which a divided (*bicornuate* or *two-horned*) uterus is one of the most common forms, have no trouble in conceiving or proceeding to term and giving birth to a perfectly healthy baby. If recurrent miscarriage is a problem, though, an operation to create a more normal uterine shape may be offered to you.

Removing fibroids

If your uterus is found to be distorted by multiple fibroids – a very common condition – it may rarely be thought to be the cause of infertility. The fibroids (*myomata*) can be removed from the uterus by an operation. But whereas they may account for some cases of infertility, they are more likely to be implicated in cases of recurrent miscarriage.

Retroversion of the uterus

Generally speaking, the uterus is tilted slightly forward inside the body, held in place by the so-called round ligaments. This is known as *anteversion*. In about 20 per cent of women it tilts backwards – called *retroversion*. It used to be thought that a retroverted uterus always contributed to infertility and women were offered an operation to shorten the round ligaments to pull the uterus forward. However, it is now thought that the uterus's position is much less important than its mobility.

If your uterus is found to be immobile on examination, then the doctor might suspect that it is bound down by adhesions from some previous operation or infection. Thus *fixed* retroversion associated with infertility might need investigation and treatment.

The operation to correct retroversion may also be offered if you have complained of pain during intercourse. This is not a direct cause of infertility, of course, but it does hinder conception by making intercourse uncomfortable and, in some cases, positively to be avoided (see page 27). If the natural movement of the uterus is restricted during intercourse then deep discomfort might result.

Your doctor might suggest that a plastic or rubber pessary is placed in the vagina to tilt the womb forward. If this brings relief, then you might be offered the operation to shorten the ligaments and bring the uterus forward permanently.

ELEVEN

Reversal of sterilization

An increasingly common cause of infertility for which both men and women are seeking medical help is sterilization. Many people, especially those who long for a child but have never been able to produce one, may feel it incongruous – even greedy – for people who have been sterilized, usually after they had had two or more children, suddenly to change their minds and want more. Nevertheless there are always going to be a small number of people whose personal circumstances change.

The object of sterilization is to terminate a man's or a woman's fertility permanently, and nobody should be sterilized unless they are absolutely sure they do not want more children. This needs to be said straight away because there is no guarantee that a sterilization operation can be reversed successfully, and doctors do not agree to sterilize unless they are sure both partners understand and accept this. However, if you have been widowed or divorced, and you remarry and would like to start a new family, or a child has been lost through accident or illness, there may be a case for trying to restore fertility so that you can try to conceive again.

When performing a reversal operation, the surgeon is faced with the same sort of problems as when operating to repair blocked or damaged Fallopian tubes or tubes inside the testis. Different techniques are being experimented with, and the experience gained benefits both forms of operation.

Sterilization of women

Three main types of sterilization are used for women; of these some are much easier to reverse than others. This is because the increasing number of women asking for sterilization has led doctors to use those methods of sterilization which also offer a reasonable chance of reversal.

The first method involves cutting the Fallopian tubes and tying off the ends, the second is to cauterize them with electrically heated forceps (*diathermy*), and the third is to block off each tube with rings or clips. This last method will probably supersede the two former in the course of time.

Chances of successful reversal

As with any tubal surgery the chances of reversing female sterilization depend very much on the amount of damage to the Fallopian tubes. For instance, diathermy destroys a large portion of the tubes so the chances of reversal are small. However, if clips or rings are used the chances of reversal are much greater – many centres are reporting success rates as high as 95 per cent. The majority of sterilizations to date, however, have involved cutting the tubes, but even here there is a 50:50 chance of reversal for women with a reasonable length of tube remaining.

Successful reversal depends very much on the point at which the tube was cut, blocked or destroyed. If the tubes were cut or blocked near to the uterus at the part known as the *isthmus* there is a greater chance of success, since the width of the tube is uniform, whereas further along it widens and it is obviously more difficult for a surgeon to join two parts of different diameters.

Using very similar techniques to those described in the previous chapter on tubal surgery (see page 96), your doctor will aim to join the tubes again in an infection-free environment with an adequate blood supply and wait for healing to take place. Unfortunately, even if the operation is successful technically, there is still no guarantee that the Fallopian tubes will function properly if the lining has been damaged; some women still fail to conceive after a reversal operation, even though the tubes are open.

However the results of reversal operations are improving year by year, especially with the increasing use of clip or ring methods of sterilization. It is possible that if IVF systems become more available and more effective (see page 102), there may be no need to perform reversal of sterilization operations. In the meantime IVF may offer some hope for those for whom reversal is not possible or is unsuccessful.

Sterilization of men

Male sterilization (*vasectomy*) is achieved by dividing each *vas deferens* – the tubes which conduct the sperm from the testes up past the seminal vesicles, through the prostate gland and out through the penis via the urethra (see page 50). It is a very simple procedure, only requiring a local anaesthetic, and has a very high success rate.

When it comes to reversal, however, there is a difference between technical success and functional success, as there is with women. The vas deferens can be rejoined, and normal sperm counts achieved. But although doctors have claimed success rates in this area of up to 90 per cent, it seems that subsequent pregnancy rates are much lower – as low as 19 per cent in some studies but up to 59 per cent in others. As with the Fallopian tubes in women, we do not yet know enough about the make-up of these tubes completely to explain these failures.

TWELVE

In vitro fertilization

In 1978 Patrick Steptoe, a gynaecologist working with Robert Edwards, a scientist, successfully delivered Louise Brown – the world's first baby produced from an ovum fertilized outside its mother's body. Since this remarkable achievement there has been considerable development of this technique, now known as *in vitro fertilization*, or IVF, and centres specializing in it have been set up all over the country.

The basic technique is simple to understand. Several ripe ova are removed from a woman's ovaries and mixed in the laboratory in a glass dish (hence *in vitro*, from the Latin for glass), with specially prepared sperm. The sperm fertilize the ova and several embryos develop. These are checked by an expert embryologist and several of them are inserted into the woman's uterus. Any unused embryos can be frozen and stored for later use. Patient and doctors then have to wait in the hope that one or more of the embryos will implant into the lining of the uterus and a successful pregnancy will ensue.

Suitability for IVF
It should be stressed that only a minority of infertile couples – probably about 18 per cent of those seeking help – are actually suitable candidates for IVF. Like tubal surgery, it is not something to be entered into lightly. It requires all the ramifications of ovarian stimulation already described (see page 86), and the crucial moment for the *ovum harvest* (collection of ripe ova) requires frequent scanning and blood

tests and could of course occur at any time of the day or night. It is an expensive process, too, (little or no IVF facilities are available on the NHS) and success rates are only 10 to 15 per cent.

You are likely to be referred for IVF if your only major problem is that of blocked or damaged Fallopian tubes. You may even have had unsuccessful tubal surgery beforehand, or perhaps ectopic pregnancies which have caused both Fallopian tubes to be removed. You may also be referred for IVF if your problem is 'unexplained infertility'. It has been shown that the chances of success with IVF in these circumstances are quite high. Several of my patients with unexplained infertility have conceived while waiting to be considered for IVF and it is tempting to speculate if being on the waiting list for IVF confers a beneficial effect itself!

IVF and male infertility
When Patrick Steptoe announced the technique was possible there was considerable hope that men with very low sperm counts might be able to be helped by IVF. It was hoped that just a few viable sperm would be needed to fertilize the normal ova in the laboratory by the IVF method. Unfortunately, although there have been some successes in selected cases and research is currently going ahead in the introduction of a single sperm to an ovum, IVF in this situation has not yet fulfilled all our hopes.

Referral for IVF
When, and only when, you have both come to the end of lengthy and extensive investigations and treatments, your doctor may possibly recommend IVF. The technique may be available through the infertility clinic you are already attending, or, more likely, you will be referred to another specialist centre. Either way, there is likely to be a waiting list and you will only be accepted if all the selection criteria required by the particular IVF centre have been satisfied.

Gynaecologists offering IVF treatment are not purely technicians who carry out IVF with no questions asked. They are infertility experts themselves and will want to ensure that all orthodox investigations have been completed before resorting to IVF. Selection criteria for some IVF centres also include an upper age limit, as the chance of success is poor for women over 38 years. Other centres only offer treatment to couples living in the vicinity. You should bear in mind that the waiting time could be as long as three years for centres attached to NHS hospitals.

Preparing the ovaries

IVF has become more successful since it has been the practice to place more than one fertilized ovum into the uterus. It has become common practice to stimulate the ripening of several follicles (see page 88) so that up to half a dozen ova can be collected at the same time.

The details may vary from one IVF unit to another but a common system would involve giving clomiphene daily from Days 2 to 6 of the menstrual cycle and then injections of FSH daily from Days 5 to 9. This will cause several follicles to swell in the ovary and these can be measured and monitored by ultrasound scanning. When the leading follicle has reached a good size, you would be given an injection of HCG for final ripening.

Collecting the ova

At the moment, collecting the ova (the so-called *ovum harvest*) is done in one of two ways. The technique originally introduced by Patrick Steptoe uses laparoscopy. Using a fine, narrow bore needle introduced through the abdominal wall, the ova are sucked out of their follicles under direct vision through the laparoscope. The procedure involves the risks – and extra expense – inherent in a general anaesthetic and the resulting physical and emotional stresses may in some cases be enough to prejudice the chances of successful implantation of the embryo.

A much less invasive method uses ultrasound scanning. Each follicle is located by the scan and a thin bore needle is introduced through your abdominal wall and into the ovarian follicles. Using ultrasound guidance, the ova can be sucked out of their follicles. This technique can be performed using a local anaesthetic, making the whole procedure a lot less traumatic. Many IVF units are also switching over to vaginal ultrasound probes, which can be placed against the ovaries, at the top of the vagina. A small needle moves forward from the probe to the follicle containing the egg, to suck it out of the follicle.

Fertilization and implantation

Having successfully removed the ova they are then mixed with your partner's specially prepared sperm. This preparation mimics the capacitation which takes place when the sperm travel through cervical mucus (see page 57). The prepared sperm are then mixed with the collected ova and fertilization is allowed to take place in the laboratory. As the resulting embryos develop, they are checked carefully to ensure they are dividing properly. Recently, doctors in Liverpool have developed a little capsule to contain the ovum and sperm which women keep in their vaginas. This keeps the nutrient liquid inside the capsule at body temperature and eliminates the need for costly embryo laboratory facilities.

Approximately 40 hours after fertilization the embryos will have divided twice and be at the four-cell stage (see page 23), ready for implantation into the uterus. Usually two or three or even more embryos are used and any left over can be stored for later implantation if the first attempt is unsuccessful. The developing embryos are inserted into the uterus through your cervix. There then follows an anxious time until your next period is due. Pregnancy can be checked using a blood test which measures the very early rise in the HCG hormone in the bloodstream.

The technique of in vitro fertilization

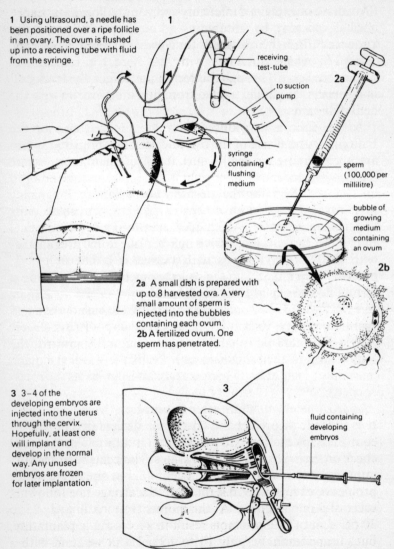

1 Using ultrasound, a needle has been positioned over a ripe follicle in an ovary. The ovum is flushed up into a receiving tube with fluid from the syringe.

receiving test-tube

to suction pump

syringe containing flushing medium

2a

sperm (100,000 per millilitre)

bubble of growing medium containing an ovum

2b

2a A small dish is prepared with up to 8 harvested ova. A very small amount of sperm is injected into the bubbles containing each ovum.
2b A fertilized ovum. One sperm has penetrated.

3 3–4 of the developing embryos are injected into the uterus through the cervix. Hopefully, at least one will implant and develop in the normal way. Any unused embryos are frozen for later implantation.

3

fluid containing developing embryos

Fertilization within the Fallopian tube

If you have unexplained infertility and your Fallopian tubes are normal you may be suitable as a couple for the technique known as GIFT (which stands for *Gamete IntraFallopian Tube Transfer*), which dispenses with the need for fertilization outside the body. Through this technique, originally developed in Australia, ova are extracted from prepared ovaries with the help of laparoscopy.

A fine tube is introduced into the fimbrial end of the Fallopian tube. Some of the ova and specially prepared sperm are then squirted directly into the Fallopian tube, where fertilization occurs, as in normal intercourse, and the embryo later moves down into the uterus in the usual way. Pregnancy rates for this method have been as good, and in some units better, than with IVF. Although there is more of a theoretical risk of producing an excessive number of ectopic pregnancies with GIFT, than there is with IVF, this is not upheld in practice. Some units have also experimented with putting a fertilized embryo into the Fallopian tube (ZIFT – *Zygote IntraFallopian Tube Transfer*) or by freely releasing the ova and sperm into the pelvis behind the uterus (POST – *Pelvic Oocyte Sperm Transfer*), where they gravitate naturally towards the Fallopian tubes where the sperm hopefully fertilizes the ovum 'naturally'.

Chances of success

It is difficult to predict the chance of success of IVF (or its equivalent) in each individual case, but most units keep a close check on their overall pregnancy rates. There has been a steady improvement in success rates since 1978, but one of the major problems yet to be solved is the high miscarriage rate following successful implantation. At the moment, approximately 25 to 30 per cent of IVF attempts result in successful implantation, but, disappointingly, only 10 to 15 per cent will end with a viable baby.

The ethical questions

IVF treatment has raised several ethical questions but not as many as those surrounding the possibility of performing badly needed research on human embryos. Doctors involved with IVF are members of the Voluntary Licensing Authority which provides an internal control of ethical standards. A committee under the leadership of Dame Mary Warnock has made recommendations to set up guidelines and controls on both IVF treatment and the regulation of embryo research. Opinion is currently divided between those who feel that research into causes of congenital diseases such as cystic fibrosis is justified on embryos up to 14 days old and those who feel that research on embryos is immoral. It is hoped that facilities for IVF treatment will not be caught in the crossfire.

THIRTEEN

Artificial insemination

Artificial insemination is most often associated with the veterinary world, but in recent years a gradual change of attitude has led to greater interest in using this technique to treat certain cases of subfertility by artificially inseminating a woman with her partner's semen (AIH – *Artificial Insemination by Husband*) or that of a donor (AID – *Artificial Insemination by Donor*).

The demand for AI and especially AID is increasing today as a result of the generally disappointing success rate in the treatment of male infertility, combined with a marked decrease in the availability of babies for adoption. It is estimated that in the United States between 6000 and 10,000 babies are now born by AID each year; in Britain the figure is about 6000 babies per year and in both countries the numbers are rising steadily.

Artificial Insemination by Husband (AIH)
One of the situations in which AIH is recommended is where a man has a low sperm count. Unfortunately the results have not produced a vast improvement in the pregnancy rate, but it is often worth a try. Doctors are working on combining AIH with the techniques of IVF in these cases. AIH is, however, of particular value in situations where the sperm count is normal but where normal intercourse is difficult, for example through impotence or paralysis. Frozen semen banks may also allow later parenthood to men undergoing removal of the testicles or radiotherapy used in the treatment of cancer of the testicles.

Artificial Insemination by Donor (AID)

AID is chosen primarily when the man is completely infertile. However, you may want to consider the procedure to avoid passing on some inherited disease such as cystic fibrosis, haemophilia, Huntingdon's chorea or muscular dystrophy. In one survey in the United States, at least 10 per cent of the participating doctors had provided AID for single women in order to 'provide natural children to women without a male partner'. However, this is still fairly uncommon in this country.

Selection of donors

The selection of sperm donors is a particular problem and the procedure varies considerably. In Britain the Royal College of Obstetricians and Gynaecologists produced a proposal suggesting that before semen is collected a potential donor should be interviewed and full medical and family history obtained, a general physical examination performed, and that he should then be asked to sign a form to state he is fully aware of how the semen will be used. Most practitioners recommend extra medical tests on donors to exclude diabetes, chromosome abnormalities, Rhesus factor problems and syphilis. Donors are also screened for possible infection with the AIDS virus.

AID is not normally available on the NHS. There are several commercial sperm banks in Britain and a few operated by academic departments of medical schools. The Pregnancy Advisory Service, a registered charity, also offers artificial insemination facilities at probably the lowest cost.

How it is done

Insemination takes place on the day before ovulation is expected, which can be deduced from temperature and menstrual charts, if you have a regular cycle. If ovulation cannot be predicted with any certainty, multiple inseminations may be made every two or three days at the midcycle time.

110

Some doctors use fertility drugs to stimulate ovulation if pregnancy has not occurred after a few attempts.

The usual procedure is to place about 1 ml of semen into the mucus in the cervical canal with a plastic tube and syringe. You would be lying on your back with your buttocks raised, and would usually rest in that position for about half an hour. Some doctors also spray a little semen onto the surface of the cervix and upper end of the vagina, or fit a plastic cap over the cervix to retain the semen so you could get up immediately. You would remove the cap yourself about eight hours later.

Pregnancy rates following AI do not seem to vary much from centre to centre, most of whom report about 20 per cent success for AIH, and an average success rate of between 55 and 78 per cent for AID, depending on whether frozen or fresh semen is used. It is pleasing to note that, almost certainly as a result of preselection of donors and the elimination of many potential problems, miscarriage, ectopic pregnancy and congenital abnormalities occur less frequently in pregnancies produced by AID than in normal pregnancies.

Psychological pressures

It is not difficult to imagine that the psychological effects of AI on both partners can be very considerable, particularly with AID. Many men resent the idea of their partners carrying another man's baby, even though the donor remains completely unknown to both. However, most men faced with this situation try to overcome their reservations in recognition of the fact that AID represents the only chance their partners will have to bear a much-wanted baby.

Doctors are well aware of the potential stresses these factors may cause, and therefore will not offer to perform artificial insemination until the couple have had some sort of counselling.

The decision to have AID is obviously a difficult one for both partners. Men tend to feel guilty, distressed at being unable to 'prove their manhood' or to fulfil the expectations of family and society, or feel that they cannot become 'a real father' to an AID child. Women also experience a conflict between sharing the man's feeling of failure and enjoying their own sense of pride. However, experience shows that most couples who request AID sort these problems out; they express a positive interest in the procedure, considering that it allows the woman to experience pregnancy and that the child will at least inherit characteristics of one parent.

FOURTEEN

What now?

There may come a time when you have to face the fact that the chances of having a baby conceived by both parents are either remote or nil. Although an experienced doctor working in the infertility field is unlikely to tell a couple that they will never conceive a child – there are countless examples of couples who produce a baby against all the odds – there can come a point at the end of infertility investigations when the doctor can only confirm that the prospects for conception are extremely bleak.

Infertility investigations can stretch over a very long period – two, three or even more years are not uncommon. Some couples will have undergone investigations in two or more centres. This is a very long time for anyone to have to deal with a personal problem of this magnitude, especially in the face of the persistent enquiries or indirect remarks from family and friends about the long-awaited 'happy event'. As the prospect of fertility becomes more remote, many couples become frustrated if their doctor's attitude is 'don't give up', so that when the crunch comes and they are told what is by then obvious, their reaction is often one of relief. Much of the inevitable disappointment will have come and gone already, long before the doctor admits to them (and to him or herself) the unlikelihood of conception.

If you feel you have reached the point of no return and no one at the clinic is prepared to give you a straight answer, write to the consultant in charge asking for an appointment to discuss the situation frankly. He or she will respond to a direct request for an honest opinion about your real prospects for the future, and should the answer be negative, then it helps to clear the air and begin the period of adjustment that will undoubtedly be needed.

Remaining childless

If you have been reasonably assured that conception is unlikely, there are various choices available. The obvious but often overlooked option is to accept 'child-free living' as it is called and get on with life. In our overpopulated world many couples (whether potentially fertile or not) are finding the choice not to have children increasingly easy to make. The opportunities for women especially to pursue full-time careers, which some consider incompatible with motherhood, are also increasing rapidly. Each year a surprisingly large number of childless couples are requesting sterilization, and doctors are responding to this change in attitude and are performing them.

I do not offer these comments as a crumb of chilly comfort to the childless. There is a growing realization in the world that the problems of overpopulation, with its associated starvation and low standards of living, must be met by voluntary family planning methods rather than relying on the old systems of population control – war, disease and famine.

Despite these considerations the average couple anxious to conceive are likely to be bitterly disappointed if fertility is denied them. They need time and support to overcome their loss, to readjust their lives and their relationships with each other, and with their families and friends. It may also help to get in touch with the National Association for the Childless (318 Summer Lane, Birmingham B19 3RL) who produce a newsletter and may be able to put you in touch with others in your area with similar concerns.

Private treatment

Overstretched National Health Service facilities, lack of

continuity, the desire for a second opinion, or simply prefer-ence may lead you to consider private treatment. This is more than likely anyway if you are opting for IVF (see page 102), but all forms of infertility treatment can be obtained privately. Consultation fees, costs of operations and the costs of accommodation in private nursing homes and clinics vary greatly throughout the country. As with most commodities, costs tend to be higher in the big cities where overheads and other expenses may be greater than in provincial towns. The most expensive specialist may not, however, be the best.

Your family doctor may well advise you and make helpful recommendations, as well as providing a referral letter. As infertility investigations are very personal, it is wise to select a specialist in whom you feel some kind of trust can be placed. If after the initial consultation you are getting 'bad vibrations' then it is better to cut your losses and choose someone else. It is well worth discussing the cost of any proposed treatment at the beginning to avoid misunderstandings later.

If you have a private health insurance you may wonder if your infertility treatment will be covered by it. Like most insurance companies, private health schemes insure against future risks which are not known for certain, but whose odds are calculable. The situation presents one or two clear facts among the complexities. If you are infertile and then register with a private health scheme and declare your infertility, the proposed insurance will probably exclude infertility treatment. If you don't declare your infertility at the time of commencing the insurance you are performing a dishonest act of nondisclo-sure, easily discovered by a few company enquiries, which will invalidate any insurance.

It would be possible, however, for an unmarried man to insure himself with a private health plan, subsequently marry and find himself or his wife infertile and the necessary private treatment would probably be allowed under his scheme. You must check with the company concerned before embarking upon any treatment as you may find you will not be reimbursed.

Adoption and fostering

When you have come to terms with your own infertility as a couple, you may consider adoption of one or more children as a way of fulfilling your desire for parenthood. Adoption is a legal process whereby the rights and duties of the natural parents are permanently transferred by a court to the adoptive parents. It is a lengthy procedure because the needs and rights of the babies or children concerned have to be taken into account first, but your local authority social services department or one of the voluntary adoption societies will be able to give you full information about the procedure.

Social services are also the people to contact if you feel able to foster children. Fostering involves providing temporary family care for a child who cannot be with his or her own parents.

The purpose of adoption

Over the past two decades, the number of babies available for adoption has declined dramatically. The process of decline was hastened by changes introduced by the 1975 Adoption Act which reduced the number of adoption orders granted to step-parents. Greater tolerance by society of birth out of wedlock and single parenthood, along with wider availability of contraception and legal abortions, is primarily responsible. Supply has increasingly failed to meet demand, especially for young babies.

With this change in numbers has come a change in attitude about the purpose of adoption. Whereas in the past the supply of babies and children for adoption may have met the needs of childless couples, the attitude is now that the purpose of adoption is to find the best possible home for the child. The time for a couple to seek adoption is probably not immediately after a doctor has told them there is no hope of reversing their own infertility. A period of readjustment and settling down to the idea may help before application is made to adopt. In addition to the normal responsibilities of parenthood, adoptive parents also have the task of explaining to the child about his or her origins. Adopted people are entitled to obtain their original birth certificate once they are 18 years of age and to trace their natural parents, but in practice very few do – two per thousand according to one study in Scotland.

Many of the children available for adoption nowadays are in the older age group, many are disabled or come from socially deprived backgrounds and offer even greater challenges which must be faced and overcome. Social service departments and registered agencies have the difficult task of assessing potential adoptive parents, and their attitudes and criteria occasionally may vary somewhat. They have to think of the future as well as the present. They need to plan for the time beyond the short space of babyhood – parenthood lasts a lifetime. It is not surprising that many couples find it easier to consider AID, or even IVF if applicable, rather than adoption.

Adoption and fertility

Adoption has occasionally been regarded as a fertility charm since following adoption couples seem to be more likely to conceive themselves. This widely held view was tested in California, but the study came to the conclusion that on statistical grounds at least fertility was not improved by adoption. An explanation for this apparent phenomenon is that in some couples conception is simply delayed for many years, and that those who do conceive after adopting a child would probably have done so anyway. However, persistent but often anecdotal reports of women conceiving soon after adoption, following many years of infertility, make statistical analysis and probability tables seem too glib. The debate continues.

Surrogacy

The term *surrogate* means a person appointed to act in place of another. A surrogate mother is one who bears a child for another woman. There is no doubt that surrogate motherhood is a very old practice. Relations and even friends of infertile women have, throughout history, given their babies to these women, and indeed there have been many instances where uncles and aunts have adopted nephews and nieces. Surrogacy is complicated by genetic paternity, that is to say, the man who provides the sperm. This can be the partner of the surrogate mother, the partner of the infertile woman (by sexual intercourse or by artificial insemination) or even donor sperm if both recipient partners are infertile.

The whole subject throws into question what motherhood really means; new terms have been coined to describe each state. There is the *biological* mother in whose womb the baby grows, and there is the *social* mother who brings up the child. The biological aspects are easy to understand – problems arise from the moral and legal standpoints.

Moral aspects of surrogacy

The word 'mother' is very old. It is defined in the Oxford English Dictionary as 'a woman who has given birth to a child, a female parent', but also adds, significantly, 'a woman who exercises control like that of a mother, or who is looked up to as a mother'.

Is motherhood the biological act of giving birth or is it the nurturing of the child to adolescence and adulthood? Must it be both? Is it morally right for the biological mother to give a child to a social mother? If after having given the baby away what if she subsequently wants him or her back? Has she any rights, morally or legally, over the child in later life? Can she see the child? Should she see the child grow up? Should the child be told of his or her 'biological' mother? Opinion on the morality of surrogacy is divided.

Many would feel that surrogacy is immoral, but speaking in a debate in the House of Lords in 1986, the Bishop of Ripon said: 'I would not want to claim that the consensus [against] extends to the total banning of surrogacy . . . indeed, even in the Church there are those who believe that it may be right and proper that a woman should offer in loving service the use of her womb to someone who is close to her.'

Legal aspects

In 1985, in a rather hasty manner and almost as an emergency measure, the Government introduced legislation to outlaw commercial surrogacy. This was in response to fears of surrogate agencies currently operating in North America setting up organizations in this country to provide mothers willing to bear a surrogate pregnancy for an infertile couple for a set fee.

The Warnock Committee made some recommendations concerning surrogacy but as yet these have not been made part of any legislation. The Government is likely to continue its neutral stance on any future legislation since Parliament and the people, as well as many members of religious organizations, are divided on the issue.

The medical facts of surrogacy

So back to medical facts. Using IVF, it is now technically possible for a woman who has at least one functioning ovary but no uterus, say from previous surgery, or who has perhaps suffered repeated miscarriages, to have an ovum removed from her ovary. This could then be fertilized by her partner's sperm and the resulting embryo could be implanted into a surrogate mother's uterus. Nine months later a child would be born who is genetically derived from the infertile couple.

And finally . . .

I hope this book has been useful in piloting you through the difficult waters of infertility investigations and treatments. Fortunately, many of you will have dropped out of the passage by conceiving a child before exhausting the means that modern medicine has to offer. If you have been lucky, I hope your attitude towards those who are still childless has become more understanding.

If you are still undergoing investigations and treatment, I hope your better knowledge of the problems enables you to come to terms with them better and to understand just what your doctor can and cannot do. We look to the future, where developments in fertility work are really exciting. The past fifteen years have seen great advances and we hope the next will be as helpful.

The Book of Genesis says: 'And Isaac prayed unto the Lord for his wife because she was barren; and the Lord granted his prayer and Rebeckah his wife conceived.' I hope your prayers are answered too.

Useful Addresses

Helpful organizations
Albany Trust,
32 Shaftesbury Avenue,
London, W1V 8E
Tel. 071-734 5588
Counselling for socio-sexual problems

Association of British Adoption Agencies,
4 Southampton Row,
London, WC2B 4AA

British Agencies for Adoption and Fostering,
11 Southwark Street,
London, SE1 1RQ
Tel. 071-407 8800

British Diabetic Association,
10 Queen Anne Street,
London, W1
Tel. 071-323 1531

Child – for infertile people,
Dorothy Bull,
Farthings,
Gaunts Road,
Paulett,
Somerset

Family Planning Association,
27–35 Mortimer Street,
London, W1N 7RJ
Tel. 071-636 7866

Foresight: The Association for Pre-conceptual Care,
The Old Vicarage,
Church Lane,
Witley,
Godalming,
Surrey
Tel. 042879 4500

Genetic counselling,
your GP has a list issued by DHSS

Health Education Authority,
Hamilton House,
Mabledon Place,
London WC1H 9TX
Tel. 071-631 0930

Relate (formerly Marriage Guidance Council),
76a New Cavendish Street,
London, W1
Tel. 071-580 1087

National Association for the Childless,
318 Summer Lane,
Birmingham,
B19 3RL
Tel. 021-359 4887/2113

The Patients' Association,
Room 33,
18 Charing Cross Road,
London, WC2
Tel. 071-240 0671

Centres offering IVF and GIFT
Queen Elizabeth Medical Centre,
Birmingham Maternity Hospital,
Birmingham B15 2TH
Tel. 021-472 1377

Department of Obstetrics and Gynaecology,
Bristol Maternity Hospital,
St Michael's Hill,
Bristol BS2 8EG
Tel. 0272-215 411

Department of Infertility,
Southmead General Hospital,
Westbury-on-Trym,
Bristol BS10 5NB
Tel. 0272-505 050

Bourn Hall,
Bourn,
Cambridge CB3 7TR
Tel. 0223-315 955

Unit of Reproductive Medicine,
Ninewells Hospital,
Dundee DD1 9SY
Tel. 0382-60111

Department of Obstetrics and Gynaecology,
University of Edinburgh,
37 Chalmers Street,
Edinburgh EH3 9EW
Tel. 031-229 2575

University Department of Obstetrics and Gynaecology,
Royal Infirmary,
84 Castle Street,
Glasgow G4 0SF
Tel. 041-552 3535

Gavin Brown Clinic,
Princess Royal Hospital,
Salthouse Road,
Hull HU8 9HE
Tel. 0482-701 151

Department of Obstetrics and Gynaecology,
St James's University Hospital,
Beckett Street,
Leeds LS9 7TF
Tel. 0532-433 144

Cromwell Hospital,
Cromwell Road,
London SW5
Tel. 071-370 4233

Hallam Medical Centre,
77 Hallam Street,
London W1
Tel. 071-631 1583

Institute of Obstetrics and Gynaecology,
Hammersmith Hospital,
150 Du Cane Road,
London W12 OHS
Tel. 071-740 3272

IVF Unit,
Humana Hospital Wellington,
Wellington Place,
London NW8 9LE
Tel. 071-580 8861

Infertility Advisory Centre,
London Independent Hospital,
Beaumont Square,
London E1 4NL
Tel. 071-790 0990

Assisted Conception Unit,
Department of Gynaecology,
King's College Hospital,
Denmark Hill,
London SE5
Tel. 071-274 3242

Lister Fertility Clinic,
Chelsea Bridge Road,
London SW1W 8RH
Tel. 01-730 3417

Department of Obstetrics and Gynaecology,
St Bartholomew's Hospital,
West Smithfield,
London EC1
Tel. 071-601 8888

Academic Department of Obstetrics and Gynaecology,
Royal Free Hospital, School of Medicine,
Pond Street, London NW3 2GQ
Tel. 071-794 0500

AMI Portland Hospital,
209 Great Portland Street,
London W1
Tel. 071-580 4400

St Mary's Hospital,
Regional IVF Unit,
Hathersage Road,
Manchester M13 OJH
Tel. 061-276 1234

Manchester Fertility Services,
Bupa Hospital Manchester,
Russell Road,
Whalley Range,
Manchester M16 8AJ
Tel. 061-226 0112 ext 332

Department of Obstetrics and Gynaecology,
Withington Hospital,
Nell Lane,
Manchester M20 8LR
Tel. 061-445 8111

BUPA Hospital,
Old Watton Road,
Colney,
Norwich NR4 7TD
Tel. 0603-56181

AMI Park Hospital,
Sherwood Lodge Drive,
Arnold,
Nottingham NG5 8RX
Tel. 0602-670 670

Nuffield Department of Obstetrics and Gynaecology,
John Radcliffe Hospital,
Headington,
Oxford OX3 9DU
Tel. 0865-817 838

University Department of Obstetrics and Gynaecology,
Jessop Hospital for Women,
Sheffield S3 7RE
Tel. 0742-766 333

Department of Human Reproduction and Obstetrics,
Princess Anne Hospital,
Coxford Road,
Shirley,
Southampton SO9 4XY
Tel. 0703-777 222 ext 8107

Other titles in the series

Coping With Children's Ailments Dr Kilya Kovar
Choosing A Name For Your Baby Edited by Suzy Powling
Counting Your Calories Dr Patricia Judd & Dr Gabi Reaidi
Getting the Best From Your Microwave Joan Hood
How To Buy And Sell Your Home Michael Stock
How To Get A Job Bill Lubbock and Richard Stokes
How To Pass Exams C.M. Hills
How To Pass Your Driving Test John Thorpe
Planning Your Wedding Joyce Robbins
The Highway Code: Your Questions Answered Wendy Goss
Understanding Body Language Jane Lyle
Knowing Your Rights: A Guide to Consumer Law Vincent
Powell-Smith, David Clarke, John Parkinson, Richard
Townshend-Smith, Christine Willmore
How To Invest Your Money John Morgan
How To Get Published Neil Wenborn
Increase Your Word Power Stephen Curtis
Test Your IQ Victor Serebriakoff
Setting Up Your Own Business Alan Pitman
Coping With Stress Helen Dore
Planning Your Retirement David Hobman
The Consumer's Handbook Jean McGlone
Writing Letters For All Occasions Joyce Robbins
Looking After Your Cat Wendy Goss
Secure Your Home Alexa Stace
Is Breast Best? Nicky Adamson
Firming Your Figure Helen Dore
Cut Your Bills Margaret Jones
How To Give Up Smoking Loulou Brown